REWIRED PARENTING

CHANGING YOUR MINDSET FOR YOUR SPECIAL NEEDS CHILD

NAKIA STRINGFIELD

Rewired Parenting Changing Your Mindset for Your Special Needs Child

Paperback: 979-8-9867785-0-1
Hardcover: 979-8-9867785-1-8
eBook: 979-8-9867785-2-5

Library of Congress Control Number: 2022947072

Edited by Anita R. Minniefield

First Printing, 2022

Printed in the United States of America

Rewired Publishing
P.O. Box 1143
Knightdale, NC 27545
www.seebeyondconsulting.com

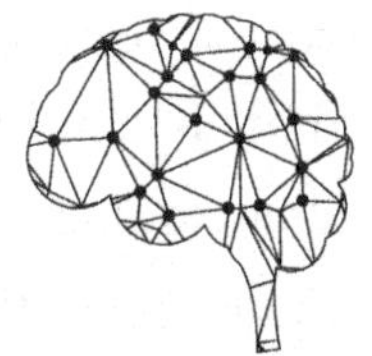

DEDICATION

To God who makes all things possible. To my amazing husband, Kwame, who always has a plan and leads with compassion and love. To my jewels, Kyra, Nia, and Regan, may you continue to shine your brilliance.

Praise for Rewired Parenting

As a teacher, professional, and social coach, I too, am a mom of a neurodiverse learner. I have always committed to listen carefully first, as families share their love, dreams, concerns, and worries about raising a child who is wired differently. Then I determine how I can support them in their journey. It is invaluable to extend grace, but moreover empower families with tools that will help them build lasting relationships with their children that will help them reach their potential! We live in a world where we get many strategies/ messages about how to get our kids to conform. The better approach is how can we build trust and resilience with the strengths that they currently have. Let's put into practice a plan that looks at the whole child, including the family—who is the child's first teacher!

Rewired Parenting takes parents on this journey by grabbing their hand, taking a deep breath, and giving them faith and hope to take the next step! Nakia's own experience has strengthened her voice and advocacy for her own children and she wants to extend that to everyone! This book is not only for parents, but professionals as well! Heartfelt and practical!

Christine Burkhart
Owner, Building Connections

FOREWARD

I first met Nakia when she reached out to me about FACES–a parent empowerment program that I facilitate for Black families raising children with autism. It was just shortly after her daughter was diagnosed with autism. From our very first encounter, I could sense Nakia's drive and determination to be the absolute best advocate for her daughter and for her family. Nakia showed up to FACES every week ready to learn, but more importantly, ready to do more for other families like hers.

Rewired Parenting is just that. This is a book of encouragement. And faith. And empowerment. It is an absolute joy to see this work come to fruition as a beacon of hope for other families. What I love most about *Rewired Parenting* is that it's not just about Nakia's family's lived experiences. Instead, it is an inspiring book of hope and opportunities for all parents—especially Black and Brown parents---to feel seen, and heard. It is a roadmap for navigating the parenting journey that comes with supporting neurodivergent children. It is filled with inspiration and moments for reflection. It is an opportunity to feel seen, but it also plants the seeds for next steps.

Far too often, the voices of Black parents raising neurodivergent children go unheard. Nakia's voice and the unique strategies she provides for navigating neurodiversity in families of color is truly what families in these spaces need. I hope that you are as inspired by *Rewired Parenting* as I am and encouraged by the boundless opportunities that come with changing your mindset.

Jamie N. Pearson, PhD
Assistant Professor of Special Education and Educational Equity
North Carolina State University

CONTENTS

THE BEGINNING

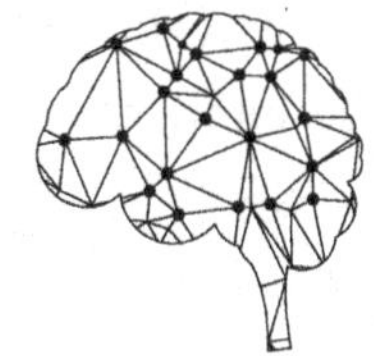

INTRODUCTION

Our journey in life is made up of collective experiences and memories. We anticipate the white picket fence, the milestones, and the joys that will be part of our path. You know those challenges? They happen to someone else. Not you. You are compassionate. You give to causes when moved in the moment. You believe that you are protected from types of situations that differ from the 'white picket fence' success. Maybe you feel you are entitled to not experience them. After giving to a cause for children or a gesture to help the less fortunate, you reset quickly. Thankfully, you shift back to your life where the stark reality you witness does not live in your house. That is until an unexpected diagnosis visits your house, your family, or your life.

This book explores what it means to have a special needs child who is differently wired. In this book, the terms "wired differently," "differently wired," or "neurodivergent" will be used interchangeably.

These terms refer to children who may sense and experience life differently than other children. These children have different brain wiring systems than neurotypical children. When it comes to the brain and nervous system, not everyone senses and experiences the world in the same way. Wired differently or neurodivergent are not terms that should be viewed as negative but ones that should be viewed through the lens of empowerment. Empowerment starts by recognizing that a new approach and tools are necessary to be successful. Children living with conditions labeled as sensory processing disorder, ADHD, autism, and dyslexia, have unique brain wiring and gifts. They do not need to be rewired. Neurodiversity refers to a group that "encompasses the full spectrum of brain differences and is made up of both neurodivergent and neurotypical individuals.[1]" The world is set up for neurotypical children and will convey a need at every turn to change and conform neurodivergent children. Through this book, we explore what it means to rewire ourselves as parents and rewire our children's environments to allow them to be who they are meant to be in the world.

This book is about bridging the gap between what we feel in the moment and what is possible. When raising a child or children who are wired differently, life may seem like the wild, wild west. It can seem unpredictable and unmanageable. It can seem impossible. However, it is possible to have the audacity to believe life is possible. A good life is possible.

This book was born out of pain and hope. I was in a place of every parent. I wanted and desired more for my children. Every parent would like to make their child's life easier than their own life. Based on your life's learnings and means, you provide experiences and create moments for your child. Things that worked with my firstborn were not working for my second or third born.

Each child is different but we were faced with schools and teachers asking us what was wrong with us as parents. We were faced with questions regarding our home environment or birth conditions that had us questioning who we were and what we were doing as parents. We were receiving calls saying "your child needs to study harder" or "your child is intentionally being a rebel." Those calls left us feeling helpless and feeling like a failure in life. This book passionately declares those feelings are wrong and not your identity. You are not a failure. Your child is not a failure. To reclaim your power, it is important to educate yourself and start a new journey! It is important to "rewire" your own programming and pioneer a new path.

As a Black mom, it was important to understand the dynamics of how race, gender, and age intersected with wired different behaviors. It was important because many times wired different behaviors can be especially misinterpreted during this gender and race intersection point. Autism is traditionally viewed as a white male condition and the characteristics/behaviors are classified from that limited point of view versus a diverse one. This misinterpretation can have an impact on a developing young mind; causing them to feel like a fish climbing a tree.

Sometimes it is important to understand this misinterpretation dynamic because a diagnosis may not be given due to these limiting factors. For example, the United States Centers for Disease Control (CDC) monitors the prevalence of autism spectrum disorder (ASD). Autism diagnoses have been historically underrepresented in girls and families of color. The good news is that diagnoses were found to be happening more equally across races in 2020.[2] In 2019, boys are still four times more likely than girls to be diagnosed with autism.[3] Even further, diagnosed girls with milder forms of autism are identified later than boys or not at all, with delays in intervention perhaps leading to more anxiety and depression in teen years.[4] With no diagnosis, teachers and schools may view behavioral concerns as willful. A misunderstood child will not be a happy child. This can mean parenting can be different and challenging as well as relationships with the school.

Continuing with autism, Black families whose children have autism and developmental disabilities were less likely to have a first evaluation by age 36 months, versus white children with autism in a 2020 study. Interestingly, in the same study, it was found that Black children experienced a 42-month delay in diagnosis even after parents shared concerns with professionals about their child's developmental skills. My daughter was 8 years old when she was diagnosed with autism. With dyslexia and/or attention-deficit/hyperactivity disorder (ADHD), the same trends of delayed identification exist in people of color communities.

Navigating this world with a wired differently child is difficult for all no matter gender or race. Discussing the micro-inequities that exist hopefully raises awareness of the need for more research, more understanding, and extra effort required to navigate this path for some. Compassion and humility are traits that we all need.

This book does not explore the depths of autism, dyslexia, or other wired differently / neurodivergent diagnoses in detail. There are many wonderful books that provide those details. However, this book focuses on navigating the journey. "Life is a marathon, and not a sprint; pace yourself accordingly" per Amby Burfoot. Some of the key resources we found helpful are included in the book.

OUR STORY

Very early in navigating our journey, I had an epiphany! It wasn't so much about changing my daughters than it was about changing me. By changing my mindset, my old thoughts, and my limited understanding, I began to realize what was possible for each child and us. It was not doom and gloom. It was about laying aside prior expectations that did not suit us anymore. Some of these expectations were based on what I thought it meant to be a mom. Others were based on what I thought others expected of me. By laying down those hard-to-reach expectations, life got better and doors opened. More importantly, my daughters were thriving.

My husband and I are parents of wired differently, neurodivergent children. We are not perfect! You aren't perfect! Guess what? That's ok.

What often felt like a split between my learnings and my experience, has become a unique perspective for parenting. As a part of my self-discovery process, I realized that my expectations were a source of frustration and discouragement. In chapter 1, you'll learn more about your parental mindset and how that is important in your journey with a special needs child.

Once you realize something needs to change, then you have the opportunity to reframe your expectations. Learning how to reclaim your power as a parent is the first major movement to rewired parenting. In chapter 2, you'll learn how you can shift from a victim to a creator view. Once your eyes are opened, it will be difficult to shift back.

Then, we tackle the other obstacles that most commonly hold parents back — fear. We no longer want to succumb to fear about ourselves as parents or about our children. To conquer fear, we start with knowledge. In chapter 3, we'll cover how to release fear and make peace with inner turmoil.

We move forward in chapter 4 to understand what your child needs to succeed. You'll learn how to connect with your child and capture the information you need.

In the second half of the book, we move into talking about more action to apply knowledge. I share how to put your tools to work. You are taking a leap of action to protect your child based on what you know. In chapter 5, we are redefining your protection stance. Most parents naturally want to protect their children. We will protect our special needs child with the tools that work for our child versus for someone else's child.

Then we look at the environments our child may come into contact with. Are we causing harm or help with these supports or places? Chapter 6 addresses how to rewire and evaluate environments that serve your child.

Through it all, basic techniques can accelerate rewired outcomes. I will summarize seven of these techniques in Chapter 7. These are building blocks that can save you time and energy.

We talk about strength for the journey in chapter 8. How do you ensure you are equipped to keep going for the sake of your child? Taking care of yourself is important. But what does it look like? I share guidance as well as some of my lessons learned on this journey.

In the last chapter, I discuss how to rewire your faith to complement your journey. Faith can give you the strength to persevere in your dark moments and rise to the peace you need for your family.

At the end of each chapter, you'll have the opportunity to apply the ideas to your own life with reflecting questions and inspiring quotes. These are short nuggets to help you rewire your mindset on your journey to approach challenges differently.

This book is for parents like you, whether you are a person of color or not. I wrote this book to be the resource I wish I had at the beginning of our journey. It is also a resource for those who are further along the way and may have had delays. This book may be a beacon of hope for all parents to encourage them to keep going. For those who may serve neurodiverse children, may this book also be a resource to help you be more impactful in your service and have a different perspective. This book captures key nuggets I learned and serves as a "thank you" to those who inspired us along the way.

I am a better person and parent going through this journey and learning from my daughters. It has been a journey of grace. I see this journey as a gift that is allowing me to grow and experience life in a way that I would have never explored. This new gift was given when I made a choice to shift my thinking and experience this life that was intentional for me to live. It all started by rewiring **my** mindset.

My hope is for this book to serve as a ripple of inspiration like a pebble dropping in a pond. A spark to keep going and rewire your parenting mindset for your child's sake. As you learn and apply new things, you can inspire others to keep going. You can inspire others to have the audacity to believe life is possible. A good, rewarding life is possible, regardless of your current situation. Having a special needs child is not the end, it's the beginning of something beautiful.

Inspiring Quotes

I do not at all understand the mystery of grace — only that it meets us where we are but does not leave us where it found us. — Anne Lamott

Hope is being able to see that there is light despite all of the darkness. — Desmond Tutu

A PARENT'S WIRING

CHAPTER 1

Many children like to keep a night light on and dread a power outage at night. Not many would desire to be unexpectedly in a dark room, unsure of their place in a familiar yet unfamiliar room. For this reason, a critical stage of building a house is to ensure that the electrical wiring is sound so that when lighting is desired, it is available. Once the wiring is there, we don't think about it unless the wiring doesn't work as expected. The definition of wiring is the network of wires used in an electrical system, device, or circuit, according to the Collins English Dictionary[5].

The human brain specializes in complex wiring. Connections of brain cells called neurons receive and transmit signals to one part of the system to another via nerve fibers known as axons[6]. Just like building a house, we don't think about our brain wiring unless it doesn't work like we think it should. How electricity travels over the wiring circuits in our brains is influenced by our programming and natural conditions. People living with such conditions labeled as sensory, ADHD, autism, and dyslexia have other unique brain wiring and gifts. They don't need to be rewired to operate in a world that orients around neurotypical behavior. However, the neurotypical orientation aims to bind neurodivergent children to neurotypical standards. There is an opportunity to appreciate neurodiversity.

As parents of neurodiverse children, we need to review our wiring system to effectively parent the gift we have been given. There is an opportunity to review not only our physical wiring circuits but our mindset. Mindset is the set of beliefs that shape how we see the world. In general, how fast or slow we process data impacts our thinking, our behavior, as well as our perception of others. In addition, our beliefs influence our thinking. Our beliefs are formed through programming by parents, teachers, mentors, and experiences. Our wiring and programming influence how we will parent or what we even believe a parent to be.

Programming is related to our mindset and wiring which will guide our thoughts and expectations. Dr. Carol Dweck[7] is a pioneer in understanding the mindset of successful people. She noted a key difference in how people approach different aspects of their life via a "fixed mindset" or a "growth mindset." Those who approach life via a "fixed mindset" seem to think if they have the skills, they have the skills. They believe they are born with a set of skills that determine their gifts. They also believe if they don't have the skills, they don't have the skills. The good news is that we know a "growth mindset" is associated with reaching higher potential and that our mindset can shift based on neuroplasticity research. Additional circuits can be built and new ways can be learned based on the original brain wiring.

Being a parent is a gift and a difficult task at the same time. No matter what stage of the journey we are in, we try to do our best. We can leverage the role models we had in our lives or other examples we see. I was painfully aware that I didn't have an exact example to replicate of a parent navigating children like mine. Initially, I didn't have a name or diagnosis to attach to our journey.

When I became a mom, I expected my experience to be like what I saw and what I heard. My strategy was to leverage all of the information I had or was learning via books to create a successful experience for our family. In my original opinion, it was important to seek knowledge, apply it, and it would yield the desired outcome. The first fallacy was believing that there was a book or person with the answers for our exact family situation. There is not. The knowledge will be built by the parent as they go on the journey. The second fallacy was believing that the "formula" would yield the desired outcome. It wouldn't yield the desired results since I didn't have all of the inputs. I had expectations if I told my child to sit, they would sit. Or, if the child "misbehaved," it was tied to a simple solution of the child being sleepy and needing a nap. Or, maybe I needed to explain the expected outcome to my child better. Wasn't it supposed to be that easy to train a child in the way they should go? Wasn't it all about conforming to a vision we had set to yield the desired result?

I had an ideology that exposure to new experiences was key to helping my child reach their full potential so I needed to expose them to multiple learnings and events. These drivers were a matter of fact and truths to me. However, these beliefs were not causing the desired result and I felt like a failure. In fact, some of the expectations caused aggravation to the very situations I was attempting to correct. I had a fixed mindset about my parenting style. I needed flexibility. I needed a growth mindset and rewiring of my parenting strategy.

There is a need to reevaluate our parenting expectations in general but especially with neurodivergent children. Elon Musk emphasizes the importance of creating "mental firewalls" to promote critical thinking and resetting of our mental operating system.[8] This applies to all aspects of life. There is so much information coming at us. How do we sort what we should believe and which expectations we should keep?[9] How do we question what we hear and see about parenting? How do we exhibit critical thinking about parenting and our parenting style? What do we need to do to be better parents?

Similarly, to Elon Musk, one of my mentors used to encourage everyone to "have a girdle on your mind." What you see and hear may not be for you. It was easier to apply these concepts to other areas of my life, not parenting. I thought parenting was something you just had. You know, that "mother's instinct" to know what to do, to be like Caroline Ingalls on The Little House on the Prairie, Clair Huxtable on The Cosby Show, or your favorite TV mom.

The mindset of your parents or grandparents served them and was based on what they knew. Your child is not the same child you were when your parents were parenting you. There are differences in the environments. Your child is a unique child with their own identity. Your child may need something different.

I was reading books but my expectations remained fixed. I was seeking information to reach the fixed expectations. I had to change the expectations and shift my perspective on how to parent.

I went through a journey of developing a mindset that I would be a curious explorer versus having a fixed formula. Through it all, I am learning to be the best parent I can be for my child, no matter what needs they have. The new "formula" is to rewire our parenting mindset. We will explore in the rest of this book how to seek knowledge about our child, apply it, observe the outcome, and tweak our expectations.

Take a moment to understand what drives you as a parent. What drives your parenting style? What experiences did you have as a child that influences how you parent? Are you doing what is expected by your parents, your memories, or your neighborhood? Are you telling your kids to clean the plate and not leave any food on the plate because of what you were taught? No matter if they like potatoes or not, you expect compliance by cleaning the plate. What expectations are you holding your child to that may or may not be realistic? What trauma do you have? What do you need to explore?

In summary, this journey starts with us as parents from the time we bring our child home from the hospital or an agency. It matters how we view our children and situations with their lens in mind. If we frame our child through our experiences, beliefs, and wiring only, this may not serve our child well. It is time to review our parenting wiring and rewire our mindset as necessary.

GROWTH KEYS: UNDERSTANDING YOUR WIRING

1. The human brain has unique wiring.
2. Thoughts and beliefs impact our mindset and parenting expectations.
3. It's a journey! Let's grow and rewire our mindset.

Inspiring Quotes

One of the most difficult things is not to change society — but to change yourself. — Nelson Mandela

I'm not in this world to live up to your expectations and you're not in this world to live up to mine. — Bruce Lee

Trade your expectations for appreciation, and the world changes instantly. — Tony Robbins

It's a good place when all you have is hope and expectations. That survival instinct, that will to live, that need to get back to life again, is more powerful than any consideration of taste, decency, politeness, manners, civility. — Danny Boyle

The sign of great parenting is not the child's behavior. The sign of truly great parenting is the parent's behavior. — Andy Smithson

Researchers are learning that a change in mindset has the power to alter neurochemistry. Belief and expectation — the key elements of hope — can block pain by releasing the brain's endorphins and enkephalins, mimicking the effects of morphine. — Jerome Groopman, M.D.

Reflecting Questions

- What thoughts and beliefs have inspired your parenting style?
- How are your expectations serving you and your family?
- What are some parenting expectations that you may want to reconsider? Why?

A PARENT'S EQUIPPING
RECLAIMING YOUR POWER

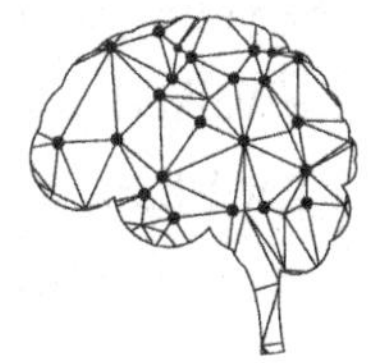

CHAPTER 2

We all have those pivotal moments that happened years ago but are as fresh as yesterday in our mind. On this parenting journey, I have had many! Here is one moment when awareness of our neurodiverse reality was awakened. This is when I realized there was a strangeness to our parenting experience. Let's go to the beginning.

It was a sunny day filled with a cacophony of sounds, sights, and smells creating a harmonious celebration of life. People were everywhere; smiling and standing in groups like corn stalks swaying in the wind. The sounds of birds happily chirping and people laughing were all around. These sounds were coaxing everyone to forget about tomorrow.

There were smells of birthday cookouts full of hamburgers and hotdogs plus fresh flowers swimming in the breeze. The sun was encasing the park in a dancing light that gently kissed your skin if you stood just right. Then, if you took a step or two, you would be in the shadows of huge oak trees giving you a welcomed reprieve to make you cool.

It was just enough and too much at the same time.

We were in the park, like others for a cookout to celebrate one of our daughter's completion of kindergarten. My husband was taking care of two of our oldest daughters and I was taking care of the youngest toddler. I gently held my youngest daughter's hand as we walked to get an ice treat where you could add your own flavors. I felt I had the better end of the bargain versus my husband as we got to enjoy a short walk and get a treat. I asked my daughter to stay by my side as I put the flavors on her treat as it was a two-handed job. After I put her favorite flavors on and turned to give her the ice treat, she was gone.

My heart was beating faster and faster while I tried to calmly tell my brain that all was well and I was mistaken. "My youngest daughter was also with my husband," my brain rationalized. I retraced my steps across the park and looked at every little girl that may have seemed like my daughter's height. I asked a park worker if he had seen a little girl walking by herself. I felt foolish asking, as there were girls everywhere, but not my preschool daughter. Surely, she hadn't gone this far. Thoughts of guilt rushed over me. What kind of mom was I? I should have known not to get her an ice treat and let her hand go. Did I want the treat more than she did? I was cold and hot at the same time.

I found my husband and let him know that our youngest daughter was lost. Another parent agreed to watch our other two daughters while we searched independently for our youngest daughter. I was frantically looking while my husband was calmly searching.

From my husband's perspective, this was a normal child loss situation and he said a prayer for help to find her. Eventually, my husband came upon her standing with a stranger near a food truck. Our daughter was fixated and fascinated by the ice cream picture on the food truck. When my husband called her, she didn't come or speak. The food truck woman was reluctant to let our daughter go because she didn't show any emotion or connection to her father at that moment. My husband told the lady that the girl was his daughter. After some coaxing, our daughter took her dad's hand after he called her name again. It was apparent that she had wanted some ice cream by her focus on the huge picture on the truck. When my husband told me later how he found her, I vaguely remembered that when we entered the park, we passed that ice cream truck. She had pointed at the truck as well as the ice cream picture as we entered. I shared that we would get an ice treat instead of ice cream since we typically avoided milk products due to our daughters having milk protein and nut allergies.

It would be years later before I realized this was a sign and part of the symptoms of sensory and eventually an autism diagnosis. The park incident would not be the first time our daughter would wander away during a moment of overwhelm, high sensitivity, or a strong desire for a "treat." The park incident began an awakening in me to search for answers that made sense. As an analytical person, I viewed this as a mathematical equation to be solved — observing the variables, inputs, and outputs in a hyper-focused manner. There had to be an answer I rationalized.

SOMETHING'S DIFFERENT

Before we had a diagnosis, we knew there was something different about our parenting journey. It seemed more chaotic and also more challenging than others. I remember talking with another parent when my daughters were young and remarking that it was easier to stay home because, by the time I was ready to leave, it had taken three hours to get to that point. Innocently, the mom asked why? I was shocked when she asked. Timidly, I mentioned the challenges of a finicky eater, multiple changes of clothes before they were calm, and how exhausted I was after what seemed like battle after battle. She didn't really look impressed or like she could relate. Inside, I was cringing. Was there something wrong with me? Was I doing something wrong? Was her experience different? Unfortunately, at that moment, I shrunk back to my inner turmoil which felt like a comfortable cave. This was a time when we didn't have a lot of friends coming over or a lot of friends to call. We were in self-isolation due to the effort to navigate work, family, and church. We were feeling inadequate. Our family dream seemed deferred if not existing. We were unsure of who we were as a parent.

We had a vision of a mom and dad with children living a life with minimum issues. This image resembled favorite pieces of our childhood experience or those experiences we saw on television that we wanted to recreate. Images that included laughter around a campfire or fishing quietly at a pond as a family. These images now seemed foreign and caused shame for me. It led to hiding and avoidance to maintain a semblance of that internal image or memory to others externally. It very much felt like this family dream was deferred.

I remember a profound loss of me during this stage. A loss of who I believed I was. This inner conflict impacted my confidence as well as my interactions with my professional work, my volunteer work, and my family activities.

When we don't have answers, we usually seek advice. When you are parenting, you will have unsolicited advice all of the time. When you are parenting a wired differently child, whether you know your child is or not, you will have extra advice. The advice will be from a place of good intent; however, it will be limited based on their knowledge of the full story. We had advice or comments like this:

- They are spoiled.
- They need a good spanking.
- I wonder where they get it from.
- The kids are busybodies and need discipline.
- You have to take control.
- You are giving them too much sugar.
- Give them some Benadryl to go to sleep more.
- You need to work less.
- Please spend more time with your girls.
- They are bored.

Some of the advice above we tried and it didn't work. We had too many voices and "advice givers." It left us feeling frustrated and inefficient. Surely, God had not given us these children as gifts for us to fail. My husband and I were both used to winning and believed that if you worked hard enough, you would come to the right answer. We were both firstborn children. We excelled in elementary, middle, high, and college academics. As first-generation college students, we believe in blazing paths with hard work and determination. What we were doing wasn't working. We were not able to solve the "mathematical equation."

We acknowledged we didn't have all of the answers. We needed a pivot but didn't know where else to go. Our family didn't have the answers. Our church didn't have the answers. Even if we thought someone had the answer, we didn't know what questions to ask. We also didn't exactly know how to navigate the feelings of helplessness. We felt like we were drowning.

As a person of faith, I remember praying for guidance in the parenting journey and how to help my children be the best they can be. I was open to information, observing others, and asked God to show us the way. We did not have clarity on how to navigate this situation. Shortly after this prayer, one of my daughters was interested in dance and I took her and our youngest daughter to a trial class.

Interestingly, the dance instructor took both of my younger daughters back to the class. I was in the lobby alone with another parent who had a 5-year-old girl sitting with her. The mom appeared to be an extrovert and openly chatted with me about her day. Her daughter was very active and had trouble sitting still. She was gliding from one chair to another chair in the small waiting area. Observingly, her daughter behaved a lot like one of our daughters. She was like an energizer bee. Buzzing here and then buzzing there. Her daughter was happy, talkative, and also seemed to not be aware of her body. In fact, her daughter bumped into me and chairs several times without stopping. In hindsight, I wonder if my observing made the mom a little nervous. However, I do not think so. I asked about the dance school and her experience. She happily shared her experience and liking for the dance school.

Then, the mom volunteered that her daughter was diagnosed with a sensory processing disorder. She said that's why her daughter couldn't be still and that spanking doesn't work because her daughter wasn't aware she was doing anything wrong. I had never heard of this disorder and I wanted to ask a few questions related to her experience. Bravely, I asked, "How did you know she had sensory processing disorder?" She told me she attended a free resource for development screening called "Project Enlightenment." She said it was a lifesaver to help her identify the needs of her daughter. She then went on to share that Project Enlightenment guided her to Occupational Therapy resources to support her daughter. I asked if it was making a difference and she enthusiastically said, "Lord, Yeah!" I was filled with such hope at her words and vividly remember this moment as a turning point in our parenting journey.

I saw the light of possibility.

Many in the Black community do not discuss diagnosis or behavior issues about their children. However, times are changing. Being curious and talking with this lady who looked like me was eye-opening. There could be a medical reason. But more importantly, help was possible. Therapy, I was familiar with! As a person who was diagnosed as needing speech therapy when I was in the second grade, I know therapy as a positive experience. I also understood occupational therapy since it was a career choice I explored before settling on engineering.

Needless to say, I soon made an appointment with Project Enlightenment to discuss my youngest daughter. Even now, thinking of that moment when I went to my first meeting makes me emotional. It was such a cathartic experience that was so full of compassion. Compassion that I was not used to receiving at that time. My counselor asked questions, held no judgment, and offered hope. She saw me and our situation fully. It was such a contrast to how I was feeling with interactions with teachers, preschools, and other community areas. I had moved from embracing victimhood to reclaiming my power as a parent.

We discussed preschool symptoms and elementary symptoms. I was given surveys to complete for determining sensory or other challenges. In the second meeting, we reviewed what the surveys indicated, which was high sensory sensitivities. I remember this conversation vividly. The project enlightenment counselor was describing sensory and asked me about my child's demeanor. She asked was my child a kind child. I was emotional and teetering on the edge of a precipice, where one feather touch would send me crashing like a waterfall over the edge. That emotion kept me from vocalizing a response and she rushed ahead. I nodded yes because it was true. She continued to rush and say good, because the loud kids, especially girls, have a harder time as the teachers think it is intentional and see the kids as disruptive. Inside, an alarm started ringing and my heart was beating faster as this was also true. My daughter was viewed as loud and the teachers were already seeing her as being intentionally disruptive at four years old. I held on to the glimmer of hope that we were on the right path although I was unsure of what was ahead in the next few months.

At the end of the visit, we received a list of occupational therapy recommendations and made an appointment with our pediatrician to further discuss. Our pediatrician confirmed that we should proceed with occupational therapy. This started our journey of a 6-month waiting period for our first appointment due to our area's shortage of resources!

While we waited, we continued to change our expectations of what a family experience should be. We resorted to reading books and websites to educate ourselves. One of the nice benefits of Project Enlightenment is their huge library to educate parents as well as children on this new world. I had never seen such books before. Based on the survey results and our journey, they recommended certain books aligned with our situation. Books from authors like Julia Cook, that modeled for children how to navigate situations and their feelings. Books that strengthen emotional awareness in children. Books that build understanding for parents to name what they had been experiencing with industry terms. Books that helped to build awareness that there was more to know.

SEEK

This education stage is important as it helps you regain footing as a parent. You are building your foundation and confidence that you are not alone. You are redefining and reclaiming your power as a parent. As a parent, you have power but at this moment you may feel hopeless. This education stage is a time to redefine your power by equipping yourself with qualified sources. You are building strength and learning in the following areas:

- Language of neurodiversity
- How to Help
- How to Recognize Triggers
- How to Recognize Symptoms
- What Tools Work for Your Child

Even if you do not have a diagnosis, there is education that is required. This education will help you know if you should seek a diagnosis. A diagnosis doesn't have to be a death sentence. However, I will acknowledge that a diagnosis has been "overused" in some people of color communities without proper support. This has led to a place of shame and also prison in certain cases. This book is written from a place of "knowledge is power." With a diagnosis, it gives a "legal" standing of your why for asking for considerations for your child. Initially, this may feel like asking for favors but through this education phase, you will understand that your child needs these considerations to be successful. You will learn to provide an environment that will allow your child to thrive.

The terminology on this journey will be a new language. From neurodiverse to sensory, to autism, to ADHD, there are so many components and learnings in the journey. Education provides a bridge to allow you to navigate to the new world from the one you have been in with your child. Just like learning a new language other than your native language, it helps to understand the culture, terminology, and practice. Understanding these aspects helps a person appear to be, and embody being a fluent, confident speaker of the language. You need to be more confident talking with teachers, doctors, neighbors, friends, and family about your child.

Some of your education will come from books, articles, conferences. Seek research-based resources and leverage material from universities or hospitals that study neurodiversity and wired differently conditions. This will help you greatly with terminology. Learning from proven sources that have sustainable track records with neurodiverse communities will also help you avoid costly sources that may not serve you or your family well. Through it all, your chief education source will be your child. Keep a journal of actions, behaviors, and observations. It will be valuable to you. Your diligence will help you to know your child better and ultimately to identify changes that should be made.

Education is not a 'one and done' type of experience. It will require a curious approach to be a continuous learner for you and your child's sake. Your children are a gift and you are empowered to guide them. You are your child's best chance for living their purpose. This does not mean you know the answers, but that you will be the chief guide to seek answers and truths. You are willing to grow and use neuroplasticity to expand into new territories. This is an adventure you are navigating. This view helps you to be insulated against the dark days and hours. There will be ups and downs, but no one is as vested as you to understand your child and expand together as a family.

Also, know that the journey is a personal one for you and each of your children. Your journey will not be the same as someone else's, although it may have the essences of others' journeys. That's OK. It is a no-judgment zone. You will need to navigate so much new information that it can be overwhelming. Remember your child is a precious gift and you are your child's biggest advocate. You are on a journey of learning to be an advocate for your child. I was on a journey of learning to be an advocate in a world where my daughter was seen as an enemy or threat. Another daughter was seen as lazy. For each child, I had to create a unique toolbox based on learning.

Through learning the language, you will also learn how to help your child with or without a diagnosis. As an example, I was able to recognize if my daughter was bluntly honest, it wasn't because she was intentionally being rude. Early in our journey, one of my daughters declared to a beautiful woman in a hallway, "You are bald! You have no hair! Why don't you have any hair?" I was absolutely embarrassed but recognized that I needed to help my daughter navigate this situation for her sake and my sake. I explained to the woman that my daughter was overly honest and attempted to apologize. The lady interjected and informed me that my child was only curious and proceeded to explain to her that she had a condition called alopecia. My daughter was attentive to her response and it opened a new door to engage with an adult in a new way. I learned through this experience that instead of hiding my child and her curiosity, I need to embrace it and explore my curiosity also. This was an example of learning how to help navigate challenging moments. By the way, I am still learning and navigating each day!

I also started to recognize triggers intentionally versus in an accidental way. One of my daughters did not like loud noises and would grunt when there were crowds or multiple types of noises. We learned she was sensitive to noises long before we understood or knew about an autism diagnosis or even a sensory processing issue. We learned to avoid certain settings, if possible, to keep her calm. We also learned she remained calmer when she was in our arms or an enclosed carrier/stroller with large crowds.

We recognized the symptoms in her body language or voice tone that indicated she was uncomfortable. As parents, we were able to navigate based on these types of discoveries and map which of the tools we were reading about to use.

Early on, we realized that our daughter liked to sleep in her car seat carrier. The motion in the car seemed to calm her. So sometimes we would take a car ride to have her get a nap. Then, we discovered that the car carrier would also work at night, like a familiar toy to ease her to sleep in particularly challenging times. We would bring the car carrier into her bedroom and place it on the floor with her in it and gently rock it back and forth. Somehow it worked better than a baby swing which didn't hold her tight. We didn't understand until later that due to her sensory needs, she was comforted by the motion and the closeness of the car seat carrier. This process is about being curious and discovering what works and applying it. You do not have to have all of the whys. Keep a journal to document your observations.

You also may not know all of the terms and be unsure of your advocacy early on. Our middle daughter had challenges reading. Through a parent's intuition, I knew her journey was different from my oldest daughter's journey. I knew it, but those considered to be experts, such as her teachers, discounted my concerns. Much later, my concerns noted in kindergarten were validated by a professional psychologist when she was in third grade.

During this seek period, we had multiple conditions occurring simultaneously with our daughters. As I observed conditions in one daughter based on what I was learning, I noticed similar behaviors in another. The intensity of the behaviors may have been different in each child. Having a journal of the situations helped to connect the dots to food, conditions, and challenges later.

Some of the terminology was easier to embrace than others. For example, I was more accepting of the term "sensory processing sensitivity" than "sensory processing dysfunction." For me, saying the word dysfunction or disorder related to an unrepairable brokenness. I learned to look at "sensory integration" therapy as a tool to help strengthen how my daughter's systems worked and to understand the inputs they were seeking or avoiding.

There was an internal battle between what was meant by the terminology and being defined (myself or my child) by the words. Words such as disability, disorder, high-functioning, and special needs were conflicting. These words are given from a view of the neurotypical lens. Eventually, I realized that the words were a marker versus a destination. The words marked the path I needed to explore to evaluate tools to add to our toolbox. It did not define us. This is an imperfect world and I must move forward versus being restricted by terminology or the world's view.

In summary, embrace the time to redefine and reclaim your power as a parent. You have more influence and control than you know. This is a time to break the stereotypes whether they are from others or from your background of what parenting is and should be. Do not subscribe to someone else's narrative for your life or your child's life. This is the time to enter the education cocoon and get ready for a later emergence. There is no wasted time in this preparation and education stage. This education phase will build a firm foundation that you will be able to stand on later. When you openly seek, answers will come. You will build a toolbox unique for your child. As parents, we become the student to be what our child needs. We rewire ourselves first by adjusting our mindset and our parenting style. This will make all of the difference.

GROWTH KEYS: RECLAIM YOUR POWER

1. Acknowledge you don't have the answer right away.
2. Cast away former expectations and tools.
3. Educate yourself to grow.

Inspiring Quotes

There is no knowledge that is not power. — Ralph Waldo Emerson

Challenges are gifts that force us to search for a new center of gravity. Don't fight them. Just find a new way to stand. —Oprah Winfrey

Parenting for special needs and 'typical kids' is like a tightrope walk without a net. The only difference is that special needs parents know exactly how close the ground is. That perspective helps us appreciate everything so much more. — Amy Kenny

If you can't explain it simply, you don't understand it well enough. — Albert Einstein

Nothing can be done without hope and confidence. — Helen Keller

I did then what I knew how to do. Now that I know better, I do better. — Maya Angelou

Reflecting Questions

- What was your first moment of recognizing that something's different?
- Where are you on your education journey?

A PARENT'S COMMISSION
RECLAIMING YOUR "IT'S POSSIBLE" MINDSET

CHAPTER 3

Once you equip yourself, there is a mindset shift that occurs. The next step is fully reclaiming an "It's Possible" mentality. What is an "It's Possible" mentality? You know that feeling you had when you wanted to ride your bicycle when you were a child? Or what you see when a baby is learning to walk or even crawl? The feeling they must have to accomplish a new task. The feeling that no matter what, it was for them. They will fall. They will fail initially. However, children have the resilience to keep going until they see something glorious happening to them. Something glorious they may have seen glimpses of in others or don't know truly what it is. It is embracing a mindset that no matter what, the journey is for you and your family. You will have an amazing journey of exploring and growing together. Embracing "It's Possible" is about taking one step to believe happiness is possible for you and your family. Happiness doesn't mean perfect. It is like a rock climber trusting a toehold and another toehold to scale a cliff. By starting to rewire your mind as a parent, you open up a new world for yourself and your family to create a spark that your family may experience joy. By rewiring your mindset and your parenting style, you become a catalyst to create a better experience for your family including your wired differently child(ren).

It's possible for you to:

- Not condemn yourself and your parenting style
- Define an enjoyable pathway that is not frustrating for your family
- See your child as a gift
- Lead your child to achieve with the right support and tools
- Realize a new normal or baseline for you and your family
- Have joy

Believing that "It's Possible" moves you from a place of a victim to a place of creating possibilities. It moves you from a place of having a diagnosis to a place of living with a diagnosis. It moves you from only seeing the challenge and feeling negative about your family to navigating the challenge and embracing life. Each of us have unique powers. This is about discovering more about yourself as a parent and more about your child than you ever thought was possible. There is hope.

Whether you have a diagnosis or not, you may be aware that life is different and challenging. You may have an internal fear that you aren't showing up as a mom or dad correctly. Or you may feel that your family doesn't look like an ideal family. Or the great fear - that it's your fault as a parent.

MAKE PEACE

You may have feelings of inadequacy but make peace with it. Don't just stay there. Feelings of inadequacy can leave you in a place of paralysis and helplessness. The definition of inadequate is the inability to deal with a condition or with life. You are not unable, you are able! The very fact that you are reading this book shows that you are able and adequate. What you are feeling and your negative thoughts are not true.

You have to shed the thoughts of hopelessness. Until you shed these thoughts, you will not be able to focus on helping your child fully. You have to shed the thoughts of "I can't make it," "I am a failure," and "this parenting is not possible." There were times, in the beginning, when I had a strong desire to physically hide under my desk or in a closet and just cry because the task in front of us seemed so impossible. We were in a place of not knowing which way to go. We would have loved for someone to have dropped down out of the sky and told us which way to go. These feelings equated to paralyzing fear and heavy anxiety.

I remember when the school called to inform us about a difficult day my daughter had. I would break out into tears when the principal or teachers called me to explain my child's behavior. I was so emotional they learned to call my husband first. Initially, this worked for me at the time because it gave me the space to navigate my emotions from the facts. I felt so inadequate that I was showing up as inadequate. This feeling and action did not help my daughter or me.

As parents, we had to realize we were creators and had more power than we felt. We could not let an unexpected condition presented by life cripple us. This was not our comfort zone but it was our growth zone. It was time to release the victim mindset and put on the "It's

Possible" mentality. It was time to pivot and create a new identity and destiny for our family. It may not look like what we thought when we first got married, but it would still be great! It is possible that our life would still bring forth peace, happiness, and joy! We were full of purpose even with this life situation presenting itself. This was not a time to hide, but to live! Isn't this what life is about — living?

So how did we do this in the midst of schools calling us for appointments to discuss expelling our daughter from school due to behavior challenges? How did we do this while working full-time? How did we do this while our daughter was facing low self-esteem and even suicidal thoughts at times?

Making peace involved speaking words of encouragement to myself as a parent first. I was faced with anxious thoughts such as:

- Why me?
- Was I deserving of this child?
- Was I enough?
- Could I do this?
- Is it possible for me to be a great mom and serve my child well?
- Will I always be in a state of limbo?

Those anxious thoughts and voices must be silenced to progress forward. I had to say countering words to reframe my reality. This was a part of releasing unrealistic fear. Fear will keep you in a self-imposed prison due to shame. It is time to reframe your vision and get free of the fears. I had to declare:

- I am deserving of my child!
- I am learning to be what my child needs!

- I am enough for my child!
- I am the chief advocate for my child!
- The answers I need are coming my way!
- I am grateful for the experience to lead my child!

By speaking out loud to myself continually, the shame started to dissipate. Part of the process was visualizing that I was able and had what it takes. Once you reclaim the belief that "it is possible" for you as a parent, then you can pass that possibility view to your child. Life becomes possible. Joy is possible. Happiness is possible. An empowered love is possible. Remember, you are your child's chief advocate and role model. Protecting your "It's Possible" mindset leads to dreaming, visualizing, action, and being. You are building new pathways in your brain and creating a new experience for your family. The self-imposed limitation of "I can't" is demolished. We can decide who we will be to our child by reclaiming our belief of "It's Possible" to have joy, peace, and life.

Part of the process also includes relinquishing envy. It does not serve you well to dwell on other families that may have neurotypical children or remind you of the old dreams you had for yourself. I remember early in our journey sharing with another mother that I admired how well-behaved her daughters were. She innocently exclaimed it is all about setting expectations and telling her daughters that they better not move. Outside I smiled but inside I cringed. I was also secretly jealous as I knew that method delivered as she said would not work for our family. Lord knows I had tried. Jealously will keep you from your reality and keep you hoping for a reality that is not your journey. Keep your "It's Possible" mindset for YOUR life.

A part of keeping the "It's Possible" mindset is to focus on gratitude for every moment in our life. Thankful if our child puts on her shoe and ties it. Thankful if we go to the store without a tantrum. Thankful if we can see our child cry and have a tantrum. It shifted the thoughts from self-criticism and focusing on what I thought we did not have, to seeing what we did have. Happiness was possible now and not waiting for something else to line up in our life. Happiness is a choice and that choice lies inside of me.

You are empowered to protect your beliefs and hope as it becomes a source of strength. When an environment for you or your child doesn't align with your new "It's Possible" beliefs, you will have the courage during this period to isolate. This is a good isolation period to allow you to get stronger. Eventually, you will start to emerge from your cocoon. Your isolation was not a prison but a chance to grow and explore. Now it is time to fight and protect this newfound mentality. Without an "It's Possible" mentality, you are in paralysis and a victim of life. You are stuck. This mentality is the lighthouse for your path forward out of a stuck state. Trust the process that if you keep an "It's Possible" mindset, you will be in a better place later on in your parenting journey. Suddenly in the near future, you will look and see a different perspective of you and your family.

Reclaiming "It's Possible" is like realizing a fluffy cloud is beautiful whether it is on the ground or in the sky. The cloud is the same whether it is on the ground or in the sky. However, the view is different. How you perceive the cloud may also be different depending on your distance to the cloud. Be curious. There is beauty in both. Both are just as magical if you change the perception that fog, a ground cloud, is bad and clouds in the sky are good. On a recent airplane trip, I was amazed to see that a cloud in the sky looked like fog on the ground. In fact, when you are close to the cloud in either location, your vision is hampered. You can't see far. Let's change our attitude. Your child is a beautiful child and your family is wonderful.

Your mentality must shift before you have a chance to impact your child's mindset. It may take time for the shift. Be patient and kind to yourself in the reclaiming "It's Possible" process for it is worth it.

E.L. Doctorow once said, "Writing history is like driving at night in the fog. You can only see as far as your headlights, but you can make the whole trip that way." We are on a course to write history for our children and with our children. Let's see them as beautiful in this cloudy, foggy journey.

In summary, reclaiming your "It's Possible," positive mindset starts after you, as a parent, begin equipping yourself. Gratitude helps you discover joy in the journey and be appreciative of every moment with your child and family. You are building resiliency for the journey.

GROWTH KEYS: RECLAIM "IT'S POSSIBLE"

1. Believe you are enough.
2. Believe your children are a gift.
3. Believe rewriting a beautiful life is possible.

Inspiring Quotes

Knowledge of what is possible is the beginning of happiness. — George Santayana

An optimist sees an opportunity in every calamity. A pessimist sees calamity in every opportunity. — Sir Winston Churchill

The wise man doesn't give the right answers, he poses the right questions. — Claude Levi-Strauss

If a man does not keep pace with his companions, perhaps it is because he hears a different drummer. Let him step to the music which he hears, however measured or far away. — Henry David Thoreau

Life isn't about waiting for the storm to pass. It's about learning to dance in the rain. — Vivian Greene

Reflecting Questions

- What thoughts have tried to keep you in a place of fear or shame?
- What are you hopeful about?

UNDERSTANDING WHAT YOUR CHILD NEEDS

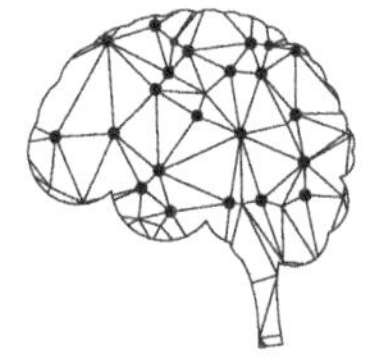

CHAPTER 4

As a parent, your chief goal is to care for your child. To do this, you must understand what your child needs and wants to flourish. Your child's needs and wants are a part of their language. In this chapter, we want to explore how to understand your child's wants and needs -- their language. It helps to think of your child as a physical seed. A seed requires certain nutrients and a minimum level of conditions to survive. When you provide a seed beyond what it needs and provides the boundaries it wants, the seed will thrive. I call this the thrive zone. We want our children to thrive! Thriving will look different for each child based on their capabilities. However, thriving is possible whether your child is verbal, nonverbal, or has different capabilities.

By definition, parenting simply means the raising of a child by its parents. The definition oversimplifies the unique relationship between a child and a parent that lays the foundation for a child's personality and life choices. Your child depends on you. No matter how difficult and trying it may be, your connection to your seed is important. Your child expects you to provide for their needs.

In psychology, Maslow's Hierarchy of Needs discusses five levels of needs. The theory concludes that the lower-level needs must be addressed before moving on to meet higher-level needs. The five needs are (from lowest to highest):

- Level 1 - Physiological Needs
- Level 2 - Safety Needs
- Level 3 - Love and Belonging Needs
- Level 4 - Esteem Needs
- Level 5 - Self-actualization Needs

The first level of needs are basic physical needs for the body to survive such as food and water. It also includes breathing, sleep, nutrients, and exercise. A lack of care for basic biological needs can increase the risk of other health factors and behavior conditions. For example, sleep is important to the developing child. Children who get enough sleep have a healthier immune system, behavior, and mental health.

In younger children, tantrums can occur when the child is hungry, tired, or missing these basic physical needs. As parents, we must provide support to ensure our children are exercising, eating, and sleeping enough for what they need. We want to eliminate this level of need from the equation of navigating this journey with your child.

If your child is hungry, they will not be happy. Sometimes children that are wired differently may not easily communicate this need or think they need food when they just ate. One of our daughters, when she was young, did not have a good way to know when she was full. She would use food as a comforting agent because she liked the textures. As parents, we had to intervene to monitor food choices, amounts, and timing. This may have included locking the pantry or packing lunches when there was no school on the weekends to control food intake.

Level 1 seems like the most straightforward level but food intolerances, allergies, hearing issues, seeing issues, or snoring, add complexity to determining dependencies or interdependencies with your child. You may need to also have the doctor do basic lab tests to eliminate concerns around this level. Take time to monitor and evaluate your child. If your child has a tantrum, is it due to this level, their environment, (chapter 6), or something else? For one of our daughters, the doctor was concerned that she was lightly snoring at night and saw that her sinuses were inflamed. He wanted us to check in with an ENT to assure that there was not anything awry. While sitting in the waiting room, I was amazed that there was a poster validating our pediatrician's comments. Poor sleep quality due to breathing issues can cause ADHD-like behavior or symptoms. In addition, the ENT doctor confirmed allergies were causing the inflamed sinuses and a cough. She had been coughing for well over a year frequently. At first, there were thoughts it could be related to Tourette's syndrome. By eliminating the inflammation from the allergies, we were able to focus on other factors.

At the second level, providing safety for your child is important. This may be as simple as providing a bed to sleep in without threat of harm. Children need to know that you represent safety and that they have safe places to go at home or in other environments. Start to observe your child. What makes them calm? What makes them relax? It may be a soft pillow or a tight corner. When you are around strangers or a large number of people, what makes them feel safe?

Eventually, we learned that two of our daughters did not do well with loud noises. It was easier to understand the lack of loud noise tolerance for our youngest daughter as she would fidget or show other signs of discomfort in such environments. The loud noise could also result in moodiness or a tantrum. In general, tantrums are one of the first indications that your child has problems expressing their frustration. The interesting part is how do you figure out why your child is having a tantrum or outburst. Be a curious explorer and observe your child's behavior and their comforts to understand what makes them feel safe. It will take time and patience, remember, you are learning a new language. After some time, we identified that special noise-blocking headphones helped her feel safe when we went to loud environments or were doing activities such as vacuuming the floor. All children want to be safe and to belong. Some kids need extra support to feel both. By understanding our children's sensitivities, we can provide extra support of their senses to help them feel safe and give them a sense of belonging. We want our children to have a moment that matters to them. Sometimes that extra support may be sitting in a comfortable seat with freedom to move more. Support may also be helping them think through a stuck situation or working through feelings.

One item that is extremely comforting to neurodivergent children is a routine. Establishing routines, that define the timing and the order of tasks, can be as comforting as a soft blanket. Routines provide a structure that allows them to feel free. Although this may seem contradictory, unstructured environments can be like free falling. We discovered in kindergarten, that our daughter seemed to get notes sent home about her behavior whenever she was in transition from one place to another or in an unstructured environment like free play on the playground or at lunch. Those times were too chaotic and negatively impacted her senses. Unpredictable inputs caused unpredictable outputs.

On a field trip to the zoo, my two oldest daughters were both on the same trip. I was spending my time with my oldest daughter. My middle daughter, who was with her class, would wander away from the class and her teacher was concerned that she was going to get lost. She was so interested in the animals and did not notice when the class was moving far away. Also, she didn't like crowds and liked looking at the animals without the crowds. I realized that my daughter needed me or her teacher to hold her hand to be safe and comfortable at the zoo.

Let's go deeper into the third-fifth levels of needs. The following sections are my interpretation of the key elements to focus on to address these needs. Ultimately, your child has a key need to be connected to you. Imagine your child silently pleading:

- Please Love Me
- Please Show & Teach Me
- Please Celebrate Me

LOVE ME

As parents, our commission is to be great listeners and be able to hear our child's true heartbeat. We have to listen with our whole hearts and yield to handling what we hear back with grace, support, compassion, understanding, and acceptance. We do not want to communicate judgment and criticism. If we do, our children will not feel comfortable with us nor will they trust us. But if we respond with love, trust, and respect for them no matter what, they will open up to us more freely. Our child needs to know that they have our love no matter what. Most children fear letting their parents down. Trust is built in the smallest moments. Do not be afraid to sit and just be with your child. Take notes. One time I was sitting with my autistic daughter and asked her what activity she wanted to do with me. She exclaimed happily, "Color with me!" She picked a page and I started to color and she said "No, no! Watch me and do it this way." She wanted to be the teacher. I patiently watched how she was creatively coloring in an interesting way with her pencils varying the intensity and movement as she went. She repeated the process and instructed me to follow her. By yielding at that moment, my daughter and I built a stronger connection that we continue to build on today. I had to take time, slow down, and be present.

Loving also equates to listening and observing. What you love, you will spend time getting to know. One of my daughters was not a good reader and her teacher encouraged her to try harder. As she was learning to read, I recognized that she was memorizing the patterns of words. For example, she would see an o as a circle. She also was winning all memory card games from preschool due to her memory. I also noticed that while she read, she would watch my face very closely for my response. I learned how to train my face to be non-expressive for our reading adventures. Although comments from teachers focused on her studying harder, I learned that she had a different learning style as well as needed support in a different way. Our love for her led us to seek and find an advocate that seemed to understand kinesthetic learning and her style. The school also provided pullout teacher support from a teacher that was knowledgeable in special education teaching but more importantly in a kinesthetic approach. My daughter began to embrace learning again with a teacher that understood her. This process started with my love for our daughter. Through a parent's love, she understood how to love herself. Now my daughter is thriving and she happily stretches herself to try out for a play, create a presentation for a class, or display her art. She found her strength and determination through her struggles with dyslexia and loving herself.

SHOW & TEACH ME

We are the ultimate role models for our children. We must demonstrate the behavior we would like for them to do. In some cases, such as with autism, social awareness deficits exist. It helps to model actions intentionally to show how to do certain actions and how to respond. Continuing with the coloring exercise, I complimented my daughter by sharing how creative and smart she was by coloring in this unique way. I described what I saw her doing that added her unique touch and value to the picture. Later, she complimented me on how I was coloring and what she liked. In that simple exercise, I realized that as parents, we have more influence than I thought, to help with social deficits through role modeling as well as role-playing. It is not saying what to do but showing by doing.

A major part of teaching also includes teaching your child how to self-advocate. Self-advocating is when your child has the confidence to say, "I need help and this is how I need help." Getting to this point, helps your child to understand more about how their brain works and that although it is different, it is not a disadvantage. This was a difficult challenge initially because our dyslexic daughter only saw her brain function as a negative. We continue to tell her that she is gifted to be able to see patterns that others cannot see. We leverage the information we learned in the Seek Phase to share with her and educate her. The goal was to help her develop a healthy self-concept so she would be more comfortable advocating for herself.

One night when I asked her to set her alarm clock for the morning wake-up time before she went to bed, my daughter advocated for herself. She enthusiastically informed me that she had it and that she had a nightly routine and order to follow. Given the work I had performed on my own mindset, I gladly stepped back and let her proceed with her process after her self-advocation. Sometimes it is not about your child doing it your way or in your timing as a parent, but learning about how your child operates. I was happy that my daughter trusted me enough to share and advocate that she had another way. She woke up to her clock ringing on time. Early in our journey, this may have been a major meltdown and disagreement of control where I was trying to force a process that she didn't feel she was comfortable to control.

CELEBRATE ME

Everyone likes to be celebrated. Here are a few definitions to review to understand the value of celebration.

> **Celebrate** — "to honor or praise publicly; to praise (someone or something)"[10]: "to say that (someone or something) is great or important"[11]

> **Praise** — "to express a favorable judgment of: commend"[12]

Commend — "to recommend as worthy of confidence or notice"[13]

Celebration of your child is a way to validate to them their worthiness to exist. It is a way to exclaim to them, "Yes, you matter! Yes, I see you!" Your child needs to know that they are worthy of taking up space. This world is wired such that differently wired kids feel that they are a mistake and don't belong. We can change the playing field for our children.

In addition, behaviors and milestones that may be easy for others such as riding a bike, or talking, can be neglected as key achievements for your wired differently child. You are responsible for shifting that mindset and encouraging your child. You can shift your connection with your child to a reinforced safety zone by leveraging the following tips. These are practices we have used in our home.

1. **Spoken Words** — It is important to use words that uplift your child. When you hear your child using the word "can't", it is your opportunity to reframe and replace "can't" with "can." Paint positive visual images to your child with your words. As an example, one of our daughters was concerned about playing her violin in front of a crowd, we shared with her that she was part of a team. By practicing, she had made progress and was ready. It was important to counter her thoughts to strive for perfection versus progress.
2. **Handwritten Notes** — Writing a note is becoming a lost art. However, it's time to reclaim it! Write a short, heartfelt message to your child and put it in their favorite place or on their bathroom mirror or bedroom door. I used these messages to simply say "I love you" or to counter a negative

thought they have heard from someone else. For example, one of our daughters experienced a time when she was isolated from others at school. She wasn't aware of how loud she spoke. Because of the "atypical behaviors" such as talking loudly, the kids would blatantly ask "What's wrong with you?" She would sadly come home and ask what was wrong with her and describe her day. So, I started to not only counter the message with spoken words but also with written notes such as: "You are loved and a gift from God. There is nothing wrong with you!"

3. **Meaningful Text Messages** — Now that our kids are older and they have electronic devices, we send heartfelt messages throughout the day. As my daughters get older, they spend more time away from my physical presence. Texting is a way I can intentionally remind each of them of their greatness and identify when they are bombarded by negative messages throughout the day. I send short messages such as "Your best is good enough." Or declare a simple "I am here" or "You are loved" message. It is also an opportunity to share an inspirational quote or Bible verse. These messages serve as reminders that they are not alone and that they are a part of a family. These messages celebrate who they are and highlight their uniqueness.
4. **Rewarding Desirable Behavior** — Reinforcing positive behavior works well for wired differently kids. This does not mean taking away awards for unexpected behaviors. That negative reinforcement or punishment does not work in many cases! We had a situation at a popular psychologist's social skills group where their means of controlling interactions was with negative reinforcement. The process included removing a star for negative behavior and no opportunity to

get a treasure out of the treasure box at the end of the session. It led to unfruitful social skill sessions and my child's self-confidence and self-esteem being negatively impacted. My daughter was not able to keep her stars due to decrements for moving in her chair or blurting out. These were the very behaviors we were hoping the social skills group would assist with through role-playing. We decided to cease support from this particular social skills group, as it did not seem suited for wired differently children. In our home, we created a "bonus buck" system, where rewards could be earned based on positive choices at the parent's discretion. This type of system must be used with care as the celebration comes with recognizing the child's choice to earn but also to spend the bonus bucks. However, the bonus buck moves close to assuming that the neurodivergent child has the skills to make it happen when the opposite can be true. The same challenges of negative reinforcement can appear if the bonus buck system is implemented harshly or focused on the parents' desires only. Other examples of positive reinforcement include giving a high five or verbal praise when your child is doing something desired. For example, if we saw our child spontaneously cleaning her room, we would take special time to remark to our daughter about the cleanliness of her room. She would strive to continue to clean her room on her own. Dr. Tal Ben-Shahar states, "When you appreciate the good, the good appreciates." What you choose to focus on will grow and increase.

5. **Clean Slate Moment** — Each day brings a new day and new grace. We reemphasized that what happened yesterday stayed in yesterday. We would not bring up past challenging behavior

or revisit it as a trend. This is a gift to our children to give them hope for today. If the behavior returned, then it is reviewed again with grace. Accidents happen and big emotions happen. It's ok to bounce back and learn as we go. I always think of Sesame Street's Elmo and Grover singing the potty-training song "Accidents Happen," to encourage toddlers. If we give that same grace to our special needs children no matter their age, it will go a long way to help them feel connected to us.

6. **Sing Special Melodies** — When my daughters were babies, there were certain songs that I sang to each of them that calmed them. Interestingly, these same songs calmed them when they were older. We made it a routine to sing these melodies and give hugs as a reminder that they are unique and special, especially during difficult times. It can be a simple tune or made-up words. The key is that it matters to your child.
7. **Create Comforting Routines** — We created a Stringfield Family Creed that our girls recited every day when they saw a certain street sign on the way to school. The creed represented our values and was an affirmation of who they were. This was a routine that solidified who we were as a family. These routines also amplified that their identity was part of the family. Other routines included hash brown and bagel day at least once a week, which we picked up on the way to school. On a week with a huge milestone, an additional hash brown and bagel day would be added. Now that they are older and we have different routines in the morning, it still means something special to have a hash brown or a bagel. It sparks memories of those meaningful, morning drives as well as reminds our daughters that they are special. Simple exercises can yield big gains with consistency. These routines

gave our daughters something to look forward to and to strive for at key moments.

8. **No Strings Attached Connection** — Throw away cultural age norms. Your child may be comfortable watching Sesame Street or My Little Pony at a numerical age where it is seen as abnormal to their peers in school. This reinforces you and your home as a no judgment zone and safe place. This is a way of celebrating who they are and what they like. Watch the shows or play with the toys with them. There were more than a few events that we missed due to clothing decision issues. Some days, the socks or panties were "messing with me." We learned to go sockless or buy multiple panties or socks that were large enough, with no seams, and soft material. In the end, it was comfort over style. This is again, a revisiting of expectations. It is being curious to celebrate their creativity if they get dressed. It just might not look like what you would wear. Stuck mental behavior may impact the ability of your child to move forward. You may not understand all of the motivating factors that are influencing them to go sockless, but don't make them feel less of a child because of it. Celebrate them and see them where they are. There may be special dress-up moments required. Include your child in the process of picking clothing and shoes. You also may need to include extra time to prepare-i.e., weeks in advance — to ensure readiness for the event. Time may be a luxury you don't have. If your child is not able to transition quickly to go to an event or through an event, ask yourself the question, "How do I honor my child's needs at this moment?" Remember, your child is worthy to exist. Parents, we have to meet our children where they are. No

strings attached connections are powerful ways to celebrate your child's existence.

9. **Surround them with Positivity Messages** — We have messages to provide motivation and support. The messages include quotes on the wall and word nuggets such as "Go Big!" These are reminders and opportunities to point these phrases out in critical moments. We want our children to be open to possibilities. Although it may be a tough day, they have support from themselves and their parents. They can "Go Big." Another idea is to connect these quotes with stories that reinforce the message. For example, we used a Marvel movie character to demonstrate a moment of overcoming the odds and to highlight that the character shows us how to "Go Big" after accomplishing the task.
10. **Freely Hug** — We freely give hugs in our home. Our daughters know if they need a hug, they can ask for one and they will receive it. Even if they don't ask, we will freely give them one if they are open to a hug. Hugs are like validation and celebration that you are ok. Family therapist Virginia Satir said, "We need four hugs a day for survival. We need 8 hugs a day for maintenance. We need 12 hugs a day for growth." [14] This is especially true for some neurodivergent children. One of our daughters would get into trouble in kindergarten for hugging her classmates. It is known that hugging reduces stress naturally and sends calming messages to the brain. When people hug for 20 seconds or more, the feel-good hormone oxytocin is released and creates a stronger bond between the huggers. Hugging reinforces your child's identity that they are not alone. It celebrates that they are worthy to exist. Note, some neurodivergent

children may be sensitive to touch. Please adjust according to their needs.

11. **Being Present** — Sometimes it isn't about what is said but about what is not said. Our daughters like for us to just sit with them whether in their bedroom or the family room. Being present allows them to know that they are important even with all of your responsibilities as a parent. Therefore, put away your phone and fully pay attention to your child for a moment. Make time for fun with your children. This may seem easier when they are young, but also important as they grow into their teenage years. Look at every moment with your child as a gift; whether you help them put on their shoes, fix breakfast, or drive them to school. As you are intentional about being present with them, they will connect with your intention and feel celebrated. Rather than your child hiding and living for others' expectations, they can feel content being with their parents. These interactions are important even if they don't have the full words to describe their thoughts, feelings, or challenges. Being present provides connection and a sense of belonging for your child.
12. **Create a Secret Place** — Is there somewhere special that is just for the two of you? It could be a spot outside or in a closet. It could also be a special park. During a particular season, my daughter wanted to meet me in "our place." It was a place where it was limited talking and just a place to be. One daughter kept books and a blanket; another daughter kept makers and a coloring book in our secret place. It was unique for each child and not to be shared with their siblings. The secret place may also change as your child goes through growth seasons.

13. **Create a Safe Place** — Is there a place where your child can go to decompress when they want to be alone? They should have a place or several places they can go. It could be a playhouse, a tent, or a corner with a bean bag. It could also be a secret place. This place must allow them to feel peace and safety. It becomes a grounding point if they have overwhelming feelings.
14. **Carry Fidget Toys**— This may not seem like a way to encourage your child. My definition of encouragement includes anything that helps your child feel safe, appreciated, or loved. From that place, your child will be brave and inspired to grow. So having toys that make them feel calm, redirect anxiety, and provide encouragement is important.
15. **Encouragement To Try** — By nature, children trust their parents and will try new ventures with simple urging from their parents. The act of their parents urging them to try shows the child that their parents believe in them. One of our daughters had reading challenges. When we went to restaurants, she wanted a parent to order for her. This act saved her the struggle and embarrassment of trying to read the menu, especially one without pictures. If a menu had pictures, she would point to the pictures to indicate what she wanted to eat. After making progress with the reading specialist, I encouraged my daughter to read the menu for herself for the first time. She hesitantly looked at me and I smiled. She smiled back and took the time to review the menu. After some time, she looked up confidently and told me her order choice of chicken tenders, fries, and lemonade. She was beaming with pride. It was such a powerful moment. Now she orders regularly and it is so rewarding to see her try new things just by reading the menu. Recently, I

asked her why she picked a certain food and she mentioned that it included her favorite fruits — mango, pineapple, and banana. With her response, I knew that she read the menu and made a choice based on what she read. I marveled at her progress, especially when she used to be restricted to finger-pointing at the pictures in the menu. It was such a joy to see her blossoming with the tools provided to be self-proficient in a task many see as very simple. Encouraged by her parents, her confidence grew as she accomplished more tasks. Slowly, we saw her confidence grow to try new tasks, such as trying out for the school dance team, school play, and even a sport she never played before. Trying out led to her experiencing failure but also success. There was a growth that occurred.

GUIDING PRINCIPLES FOR PARENTS

Parents need to use guiding principles to help provide boundaries for their child to thrive. These principles ground your thoughts to help you continue to provide what your child wants and needs. I would use these almost like a warning to myself to ensure we were moving in a positive way. These principles help you to be a better advocate on behalf of your child at home, school, or other places The guiding principles are:

1. **Don't assume I understand** (I might not understand although it may look like I do)
2. **Don't rush me** (Please be patient with me)
3. **Don't hide me** (Please help me make friends and shine)

DON'T ASSUME I UNDERSTAND

This first guiding principle may be a paradox. In the physical, a child may be in the 90+ percentile for height and weight at their age, but mentally do not understand in the 90+ percentile range. Understanding is not the same as measuring intelligence. Frameworks of determining understanding ranges are limited and based on neurotypical guidelines. As a human race, we have implicit biases to lean to assumptions by extending what a person looks like in one area to all areas. These gross assumptions can impact our neurodivergent children. It is also proven that cultural bias exists that may disproportionately impact population segments such as Black girls. Research has shown Black girls are viewed as more adult-like. This can lead to Black girls being seen as needing "less nurturing, protection, and support than their peers."[15] These are factors to be aware of as you advocate on behalf of your child.

Although it may appear that your child understands, they may not understand. They need you to help them understand. They need you to expose them to things. They need you to model a growth mindset. They simply need you! You may think by sharing with your child once how to keep their toys in a certain place that no further instruction is needed. However, they may not understand and may need instruction differently. Even if your child says, "Yes, I understand" or is silent when you asked, they may not understand. You may have to go the extra mile to provide examples or references from videos, movies, songs, or prior experiences you all have shared to provide clarity. This exercise may need to happen multiple times. This will require lots of patience.

Girls may be great mimics with autism. They can observe until they learn the "rules" and then imitate their way through social scenarios without truly understanding. We had challenges navigating social scenarios. During a swim meet, the kids were telling jokes and laughing. My daughter was not aware of the meaning of the jokes but laughed as they were calling her names. This was a time when she wanted friends and was willing to do what she thought was the behavior that would have peers like her. This situation occurred before we had an autism diagnosis, but through observing my child and the situation, I was able to intervene and removed her from this situation.

Discipline is an important area where it is crucial to be tuned into your child. Your child is not you. As we went through social skills training, I realized that my child was misreading or missing others' facial expressions, mannerisms, and words. My child truly did not understand how her words, tones, or volume were impacting others. So how could I discipline my child in a traditional way when they truly did not understand? It made a world of difference to attend social skills training to help my child understand her emotions, recognize her levels, and how to navigate. It can take an ADHD/autistic child hours to get "unstuck" from a challenging moment. Many times, outbursts are outcomes of a defensive, stuck, overwhelmed mindset. Your child may lack the skills to communicate their feelings or frustrations at the moment. The mental and physical chemical reactions may be overwhelming.

We had to help our daughters' teachers understand that there was a perception gap in what was being asked. We always have to keep that in mind when disciplining, to ask our daughters more questions around the following:

- Why are you doing this right now?
- What is bothering you specifically?
- What don't you like about what I am saying?

Disciplining can't happen without understanding by both parties — parents and child. Also, your child may not be at a development level to answer the questions above, no matter what their age or size. It will take patience. The definition of disciplining includes the following:[16]

- To punish or penalize for the sake of enforcing obedience and perfecting moral character
- To train or develop by instruction and exercise, especially in self-control
- To bring under control

The second bullet is in line with my current belief related to discipline. It should be a means to help a child understand and develop. However, if a child doesn't understand their feelings or how to navigate those feelings with self-control, should discipline happen? Traditional discipline (bullet 1) assumes that the child understands and is willfully not complying with the rules. Many times, the opposite is true. The child is trying and may not have the skills to comply as requested.

This applies also to discipline in schools. Thought should occur before removing a child from an activity like recess or a fun activity. If there is no understanding by the child of why, it does not serve a purpose for the child.

As an example, my daughter desired to be in the elementary school play as a part of her theater elective. Because of her restlessness, she was having some behavior challenges in class and the theater teacher thought my daughter would get off base and act defiantly at times. She was on a probation period and at risk of being removed from the play. Initially, the theater teacher thought my daughter was intentionally misbehaving and a disciplinary challenge.

Through a partnership with the teacher, we discussed strategies to keep our daughter engaged and focused during the rehearsals. Although my daughter liked the play, she was "bored" at times, and sometimes she didn't understand what was being asked of her. We would coach our daughter at home and sometimes she got it and other times she didn't. However, we didn't stop coaching and listening. We told her to squeeze her muscles and see how high she could count each day while she waited for her part. In occupational therapy, we learned about the power of activating her muscles to help her focus. Our therapist also encouraged us to make it a game as our daughter was competitive. So, my husband challenged my daughter to count higher each day. It was working, but my daughter was still in the probation period due to the rough start. In addition to the squeeze technique, she developed another strategy to keep focus. To keep herself entertained during rehearsals, she learned all of the parts of her classmates. She memorized everyone's lines and acting parts. Shortly after a few practices, she could quote any part of the play at will and would frequently act out her favorite parts in front of anyone willing to listen.

Another teacher was aware of my daughter's sensory and attention issues but also noticed her memorization strengths. She advocated for my daughter to take on a larger role. When the student playing the scarecrow got extreme stage fright and didn't know the lines, my daughter was tapped to play the scarecrow the day before the event. She wasn't frightened. She performed her role as a dancing flower and the speaking role of the scarecrow with joy in the elementary Wizard of Oz play.

Amazingly, she went from being viewed as a contrary student to being viewed as a crucial student. She saved the play! The theater teacher was happy because the play was able to be performed as designed with the intended characters and flow. My daughter's ability to memorize all the lines and parts by watching her classmates practice was unique.

Her strength to remember the lines of the characters was an asset in the play. Showcasing her strength also allowed her confidence to bloom. She was needed and one of the stars of the show. She no longer felt like she was a pest to her teachers. After the show, the theater teacher celebrated my daughter for being a "special, bright, and talented girl" and declared she was "the best scarecrow ever." The teacher also thanked my husband and me for "being such a strong voice" for our daughter. If my child had been removed from the play rehearsals at the beginning, the benefits to the child and the community would have been lost.

The goal is to be an advocate for your child when it may look like your child understands but doesn't. Your role can be the bridge needed to help them to be understood. Your role will also help your child grow in confidence and understand their strengths.

DON'T RUSH ME

The second guiding principle focuses on being patient. Your child needs you to not rush them. I learned that my children needed extra time to process and I needed to be patient. This will be challenging but crucial. Exercise your patience.

Two of our daughters' experienced nightly bedwetting well beyond the toddler stage. Initially, we tried to encourage them to wake up and even said harmful words like "You are old enough not to wet the bed. Try harder." We pursued modifying the nightly routine, using timers, body alarms, and adding medication to help. Initially, our approach and words were based on rushing our daughter based on perceived norms. We also wanted this stage of washing sheets and wet beds to be over. We adapted to where our child was by adding the help plus waterproof mattress protectors.

Some neurodivergent children may need extra processing time for completing activities or tasks. It is easy to assume, based on neurotypical standards, that a child may be intentionally forgetting to do chores or wasting time while doing homework. However, to shine, your child may need to invest extra hours in reading and homework exercises. This is not a time to incorrectly discipline a child or to assume the child is lazy. Support your child's resiliency; determine the parameters needed for their success. Do not hold your child to neurotypical time standards. Your child may need accommodations to existing processes for success based on their unique wiring. This may mean seeking an allowance for your child to have extra time on tests or for projects. It may include a quiet, isolated space for taking a test so they can focus on the test and not on other kids.

If your child is a teenager and loves children's programming, it's ok. This may be an example of delayed executive functioning[17]. It has been identified that the mental maturity of neurodivergent kids compared to neurotypical kids, can appear 2-3 years delayed. Delayed executive functioning in children may look like challenges with understanding the passing of time and doing tasks they don't want to do. It also can look like delayed social interactions. Looking at children's programming may feel more comfortable for a neurodivergent teen versus looking at a teen TV show. When we had outings for our daughters with friends or family members, sometimes they would be more comfortable with younger children or younger children's activities. We did not shame our daughter because a friend of the same age is looking at a teen show and she is looking at Sid the Science Kid. We may need to encourage her and protect her from criticism from the "friend."

Extra supports are important versus rushing your child. When my daughter was the flower girl in a wedding, we practiced walking down the aisle and the tasks she was to accomplish. Apparently, it wasn't enough practice nor was she expecting a large number of people at the wedding. When it was time to walk down the aisle on the day of the wedding, she froze and was standing still at the end of the aisle. One of the groomsmen saved the day by thinking quickly. He kneeled on one knee and beckoned her to come with his hand. She didn't drop one flower petal walking down the aisle but she did walk slowly down the aisle to the groomsman. In her moment of overwhelm, she needed time to process but also a cue to get unstuck. Thankfully, both of those worked on the day of the wedding.

Another tool is to be patient and use "I trust you" language with your child. Using "I trust you" language, places control and accountability on the child. This means that you are also vested to provide the support that they need and to step back. As an example, I told my daughter, "I trust you to wake yourself up in the morning with your alarm clock." Then, I must be patient as she adjusts to using the clock and waking herself up. I would set my alarm to go check on her 5-10 minutes after her alarm went off. Then, I would remind her "I trust you to wake yourself up." It was hard because I was desiring to command her to get up and get moving so we wouldn't be late. However, she needed processing time and time to grow into her own routine.

The goal is to build trust with your child. This will allow them to grow and experience new adventures safely. It will not be easy but worth it.

DON'T HIDE ME

The third principle addresses helping your child shine socially and outside of your home. Your child may feel isolated and will need your help to change that perspective. First, help them be a part of social activities such as swimming, Scouts, martial arts, or dance. These activities will help them integrate and have social events. It is usually better to have them engage in activities that are individual in nature but also provide a sense of community. A community that is accepting of differences is important and we will cover more about what an accepting environment looks like in the next chapter.

Second, expose your child to others who have differences that are similar to theirs. Your child may be familiar with feeling rejection, but now we have an opportunity to create a sense of belonging with peers. In elementary school, I was able to identify parents of wired differently kids usually at school events and we would somehow bond. This allowed us to encourage our children to play together or support each other. We would often share tips, resources, or encouragement with each other.

As your child gets older, it remains important to help them find the right peer connections. Their relationships with friends become an important source of self-esteem and support. The right community will help them to realize they are not broken and to embrace their identity in a positive way. We also shared online videos of wired differently kids sharing their positive stories of navigating school and life.

In summary, your role is a powerful one for your child. By embracing the knowledge that your actions greatly affect your child, the challenges of taking care of your child are easier to solve. Instinctively, your child will trust you because you have been their safe place. When your child was scared, you held them. When your child was hungry, you fed them. You are your child's lifeline. You are all your child has and will be looking to you for guidance. Therefore, there is a responsibility to watch how you respond to your child's actions and lack of actions. Don't violate your child's trust as you navigate this parenting journey. Be careful in times of frustration not to crush or misuse their trust. Continue to show empathy to your child. Your response matters greatly.

Learning about a study solidified my understanding of the importance of my role to influence my child with my response. A scientific experiment determined babies had depth perception based on how they responded to a visual illusion of a cliff drop. The crawling baby would be safe but could sense the drop. When they were near the edge of the cliff, their heart rates raced, their eyes widen, and their breathing rates increased[18]. Joseph Campos expanded the experiment to investigate the role of a mother's facial expression to provide clues for the baby on what to do when faced with the unknown[19]. When the baby crawled to the edge of the visual cliff, the mother would make either a fearful face or an encouraging face. In most cases, the baby responded to the fear face by choosing not to cross the visual cliff. Those that were encouraged, crossed the visual cliff.

The experiment shows how important a trusted parent's encouragement is to a baby. It helps the baby to move forward in an uncertain situation. This is the same for our special needs parenting journey.

Being a parent is rewarding and you can have less frustration with how your child is progressing versus another child. I remember looking at other parents and wondering why my child isn't doing the same as theirs. Your child's progress may grow inch by inch. Gradual and slow. You set your expectations for expertise in caring for your child. If anyone can find the answer to what is best for your child, you are the one.

There is a culture that seeks to rewire the child. They think that the neurodivergent child is broken. Our child is not broken. Society is broken when it doesn't know generally how to handle a non-typical child. Let's rewire our brains as parents so we can help our children soar and be uniquely them.

One day after taking my child to the children's museum for a play date, I stood back and marveled. Here was my child standing still and observing what was happening and deciding where she wanted to join in. She wasn't the energizer bee bumping into others and zooming around frantically. She wasn't unsure of where she belonged or who she was. She wasn't screaming at others to stop looking at her. She wasn't hiding under a chair. She seemed at peace. She was happy. She was thriving. She had friends. She was uniquely her.

This example was not a fluke. At the end of another daughter's eighth-grade year, I also marveled. She navigated dyslexia/ADHD to share her gifts of art, dance, and time with the world. She was bold to share her voice, prioritize her time, and seize opportunities. My daughter's works were celebrated. Her success was recognized beyond her family and in her community. She was making friends and she was at peace being herself. She was no longer hiding and playing small.

GROWTH KEYS: UNDERSTANDING YOUR CHILD

1. You are the expert on your child's needs.
2. Progress is Progress. Celebrate it all!
3. Ground your thoughts to help your child thrive.

This success was possible by intentionally focusing on understanding our children. We celebrated all progress even if it was an inch. Hold on to hope. Your success with your child may look different. The ultimate success is when your child is at peace and blooming. The other milestones are the overflow from that inner peace.

Inspiring Quotes

Don't think that there's a different, better child 'hiding' behind the autism. This is your child. Love the child in front of you. Encourage his strengths, celebrate his quirks, and improve his weaknesses, the way you would with any child. You may have to work harder on some of this, but that's the goal. — Claire Scovell LaZebnik

Focus more on who your child is than on what your child does. Remember, you're growing a person, not fixing a problem. — L. R. Knost

Why fit in when you were born to standout. — Dr. Suess

If you've met one individual with autism, you've met one individual with autism. — Stephen Shore

There needs to be a lot more emphasis on what a child can do instead of what he cannot do. — Temple Grandin

A child with autism is not ignoring you; they are simply waiting for you to enter their world. — Unknown

Motherhood is about raising and celebrating the child you have, not the child you thought you would have. — Joan Ryan

Our children need to grow up with the awareness that who they are is worthy of celebration. — Dr. Shefali Tsabary

Children are apt to live up to what you believe of them. — Lady Bird Johnson

My mission in life is not merely to survive, but to thrive; and to do so with some passion, some compassion, some humor, and some style. — Maya Angelou

Reflecting Questions

- What perspective about your child has shifted?
- What ways have you celebrated your child?
- What way will you add to your toolbox to celebrate your child?
- How do you communicate your child's value?

A PARENT'S ADVOCACY
REDEFINING YOUR PROTECTION STANCE

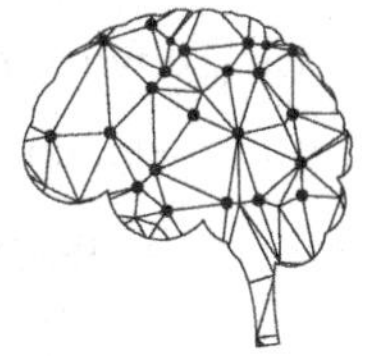

CHAPTER 5

Your goal is to protect your child so they can live, grow, and thrive. The ultimate goal is advocating for your child and creating a space, a grace bubble, that allows them to have room. This grace bubble allows them to have room to make mistakes. It allows them to navigate with a necessary cushion to their self-esteem and confidence. This room allows them to build resilience. This grace bubble allows them to survive but more importantly to thrive. Visualize your child as a seed within this grace bubble, surrounded by protection. To do this effectively, you must understand your child's needs and wants.

There are a few definitions we should visit to help understand our role to advocate with grace and protect our children.

> **Resilience** - an ability to recover from or adjust daily to misfortune or change[20]

Grace - ease and suppleness; favor[21]

Advocate - to speak or write in support of; be in favor of[22]; one who pleads the cause of another[23]

I am learning much about grace as a mom of wired differently children. Initially, my autistic child didn't get much grace in navigating environments on her own. Once I was aware of her diagnosis and started educating myself, I learned to fight for some grace room and to be resilient in the fight. Grace advocacy is the opposite of quick time. It is like slow cooking in a crock pot. The process is like the slow heating of gold. With patience and room, the savory flavors will be evident and your child's brilliance will shine.

Advocacy at times will appear controversial. It is. You are fighting for your child just like a lawyer pleads the case for their client. It is not a given that everyone will understand the case as it is presented. As the lawyer learns new information, the case can be strengthened and adjusted. The lawyer knows their client is valuable and believes in their cause. The lawyer is not trying to change the client but is advocating for them.

Being wired differently makes some things others find easy, difficult. It also makes some things others find difficult, easy. When observing an Android phone and an iPhone, both have similar functions but have different behaviors to accomplish these functions. Certain functions are done differently on one phone than the other. Understanding that the wiring design is different alleviates the frustration of expecting an Android to operate exactly like an iPhone or vice versa. Both phones are beneficial and valuable.

As it is with our children. It is important to learn our children's language and wiring to help them understand that there are benefits and purposes to their wiring although it may be different from others' wiring. Science is beginning to understand and embrace the remarkable advantages of having a differently wired brain. Research continues to evolve; highlighting the different, valuable ways of thinking. It is recognizing that our neurodivergent children may express themselves in creative ways or need different stimuli for learning to happen.

My saving grace has been to nurture my children's gifts. I learned about their strengths with diligence and through education. This is a continual learning journey as their strengths and interests may evolve. Nurturing their gifts has been an important act at times more than nurturing their struggles. This is not easy because many times our children struggle with behaviors or areas where society judges them. For example, your child may struggle with doing well in school. We took a stance to de-prioritize making A's and focus on doing your best. I tell my dyslexic daughter that her brain prefers to learn with different materials than the schools use at times and there isn't anything wrong with that. It just means sometimes we may have to take a different path to support. Dyslexic thinking is now defined in Dictionary.com and recognized by LinkedIn due to the creative and problem-solving strengths it brings.[24] Dyslexic brains are wired differently and process information differently. This genetic difference empowers dyslexics to be visual-based thinkers and great problem solvers. Although they may have challenges with traditional ways of learning and reading, dyslexics may excel in math and science due to their thinking style. They also have a higher level of work ethic since they usually work much harder and longer than their peers. Interestingly, 35% of US entrepreneurs have been identified to be dyslexic.[25] Sharing this scientific information helped us empower our daughter with her strengths.

A key part of reclaiming your protection stance as a parent is to see your child as a seed. In the last chapter, we reviewed what is unique about your seed and how to understand your seed. This chapter is about reclaiming your parental position to protect. It is like putting on the armor knowing that a battle is coming or that the battle is here. This is about asking yourself the question "How do I use what I know about my child to protect my child."

You are going to put to work the tools you learned through your education journey. As an example, sensory processing can be independent but also codependent with autism. As parents, we provide extra support to their senses to feel safe. This allows them to have a moment that matters to them. Sometimes that extra support may be headphones to help them not be jumpy or scared of loud music at an event. Or they may need headphones to help them feel empowered to complete chores like vacuuming their bedroom. Other times, we may need to sit in the back of the church to allow them the freedom to move more. Or we may need to be more patient to allow them to think or breathe through a stuck situation. Other wired differently parents are on a similar journey that may look different for each child or family.

Tools may include therapy intervention, medical intervention, or structures such as IEP/504 Plan. These tools are ways that you add protection for your child in various conditions. You can integrate these mechanisms based on your knowledge of your child.

Some of us have been taught that having an IEP (Individualized Education Plan) is bad. I was concerned about labeling my child with an IEP or as a special needs student. However, I started to look at the IEP as a way to inform the education system of the structure and boundaries that my child needed to be successful. It is a way to determine measurable and attainable goals that alleviate our child's frustration and help them soar. It is a way to provide them with some grace room.

To avoid being overwhelmed and to provide the best protection for our child, we hired a parent advocate to help us navigate the system effectively. As working parents, we did not know the laws or systems and what was our right to ask. Naively, we assumed that the school would offer the help our child needed. The school is a team with the parents but will not know your child's needs as well as you do. If you can't afford to pay for an advocate, there are community support advocates who may be willing to help by reviewing your situation, existing IEP, or needs.

The parent advocate was the voice we needed to lead us through the interactions with our daughter's school confidently and in an unemotional way. We were still dealing with the new diagnosis, behavior challenges, and so much uncertainty. We realized that our advocate was a trusted member of our team to help us to:

1. Document facts
2. Proceed with reasonable next steps based on facts
3. Evaluate the child's school environment
4. Show up professional
5. Advocate for our child's needs

Our advocate helped us to navigate and determine if we were moving in the right direction. Due to our advocate's experience, we were able to determine when we needed to ask for a functional behavior assessment, a behavior intervention plan, or a change of course. As a bonus, a solid advocate also has an extensive list of resources as well as tips. These tips saved us time and money. From a time, perspective, there is evidence of children aging out of the public school system before they have the support they need. So, creating the right structure of support quickly can prevent delays that can have other negative side effects. Through an advocate, you may be able to get a quicker connection to a doctor or service aligned with your needs.

Medicines — traditional or non-traditional— can be a way to help your child navigate certain environments and regulate their feelings. It is not a way to change your child into a neurotypical child. Pursuing holistic and medical enablers to help the ADHD and differently wired mind is a personal one. Regardless, get as much information as possible and move forward gently. This can be an important part of your toolset.

Another way to protect your child is by changing expectations. Know that changing expectations is necessary and is a way of protecting your child. What may have been "normal" for another child or another family, may not be normal for your family. You may need to change your expectations and provide protection for your child.

Some of the ways to advocate for your child may include how you:

- Say no to participating in certain events
- Avoid certain birthday parties
- Limit family gatherings and playdates
- Provide more structure to your home environment
- Limit anxiety by creating predictable events
- Sit in certain locations (side or back) to allow flexibility
- Modify family schedules

As an example, depending on the timing of the birthday party invite, we, as a family, may avoid the party or ensure there were naps in place for the children before the party. Even with these pre-event steps in place, we needed to be prepared to be flexible and leave if the environment was not conducive to our family's needs. This may seem frustrating if you want to be at a family Thanksgiving event and need to leave early to protect your child. However, what are you saying to your child if they are crying and overstimulated? We don't want to force our children to be overstimulated extensively. There were times that I would sit in the car with my child, at a family celebration, to allow some space and opportunity to calm or cool down due to sensory sensitivity.

Sensory processing challenges are real challenges. Your child may not like certain textures of foods, clothes, loud noises, or crowds. You may need to be sensitive and change your expectations of what a holiday celebration looks like. Your child may not love your favorite food dish because of how it feels, tastes, or looks. Do not get mad. You may consider buying different types of materials or foods that you are not familiar with.

Changing my parental expectations requires a continual revisit. As a first-generation college student, I understood the importance and power of exposure to spark possibilities in the lives of youth. So, for me, that evolved into a comprehensive list of technology and art camps during the summer for our children. Maybe my child didn't need to go to a different camp every week as the variety was causing unnecessary stress versus the inspiring challenge that I desired each child to have. Although I wanted to ensure my child understood commitment and the connection of hard work with results, maybe it was ok to skip a swim practice due to my child having a challenging day. Maybe it was ok to have a quiet weekend at the beach versus visiting family and friends. Maybe it was ok to just sit on the couch and snuggle while watching a funny movie together. It may mean being sensitive enough to explain a little more. Differently wired children may be very literal and have a difficult time understanding jokes, getting sarcasm, and reading between the lines. So, this rewired parenting journey will require more patience and resilience.

In a cooperative environment, advocating works well when you tell others what you need and what your child needs. For example, when we understood sensory processing disorder, we explained to caregivers, that certain food textures or clothes textures bothered one of our daughters. By sharing information with our caregivers, there was an empowerment that we were embracing to protect our child from being misunderstood. In another example, one of our daughters spoke loudly and was not aware that she spoke loudly. Once we were aware, we used occupational therapy to help, but also ensured that we shared this information with appropriate caregivers. Although she still speaks louder than other kids in certain situations, progress has been made. We have shared knowledge with her teachers to continue to make progress, but also to avoid misunderstandings.

In a non-cooperative or rigid environment, we defended our daughters' needs aggressively to counter continual misunderstandings and assumptions. We needed to protect our children. Changing expectations started with us. Then, we needed to influence the expectations of others that interacted with or taught our children.

Ultimately, self-advocacy is the goal for our children. Our daughter, who is dyslexic, had challenges with reading. She had been empowered with tools to help her to keep pace and assist her reading. When there was an announcement to join a school book club during lunch, she was interested, especially since her friends were going. However, her first concern was if she would have to read out loud in front of the club. She asked her teacher and discovered it was a book discussion club. She requested an audible program to read the book to herself at home to keep up with the pace of the book club's assignments. She was able to actively participate in the book club discussions with her friends and share her point of view. It was an eye-opening experience for us to see her advocate for herself and to choose the tool she needed to participate. She enjoyed "reading" a book that was engaging and discussing it with her peers. It boosted her self-confidence. She then asked us for the audible version of the sequel book to read on her own.

In summary, you must make a decision and move and shift as you need to. All of it is learning. Be open and flexible to apply what you are learning about your child to help protect them. Protecting your child includes putting new tools to work as you observe and learn more about your child. You know more about how to fight and advocate for your child. Your child is worth it.

GROWTH KEYS: RECLAIM YOUR PROTECTION STANCE

1. Be a grace advocate.
2. Wield your tools.
3. Change your expectations.

Inspiring Quotes

The definition of insanity is doing the same thing over and over and expecting different results. — Albert Einstein

If they can't learn the way we teach, we teach the way they learn. — Dr. O. Ivar Lovaas

Once you choose hope, anything's possible. — Christopher Reeve

Children need at least one person in their life who thinks the sun rises and sets on them, who delights in their existence and loves them unconditionally. — Pamela Leo

Mild autism doesn't mean one experiences autism mildly. It means you experience their autism mildly. You may not know how hard they've had to work to get to the level they are. — Adam Walton

Everybody is a genius. But if you judge a fish by its ability to climb a tree, it will live its whole life believing it is stupid. —Unknown

Reflecting Questions

- What expectations do you have that may not be working for your child?
- What tools do you have in place?
- What tools are you willing to explore more?

REWIRED ENVIRONMENT IT MATTERS

CHAPTER 6

This chapter deals with how to ensure your child's environment has what is needed to allow your child to grow inside and outside of the home. Now that you understand your child's needs, you must evaluate the environments that support your child against their needs. Your child is a seed that will flourish in the right environment or wither in the wrong environment. Once you know the non-negotiable characteristics of your child, you can guide your child to advocate for themselves. Also, note that these characteristics may change over time. This is about your child understanding their strengths as well as their nonnegotiable. For example, my daughter knew, based on her writing and needs, that she needed extra time to do her best on tests. It helped her to have extra processing time and quiet spaces, especially on key tests. If she needed support, she knew how to ask for extra time from her Special Education teacher and where to go to take the test according to her IEP. I did not have to coordinate with her teacher.

When we teach our children to advocate for themselves, we are teaching them to be leaders. If they are not able to advocate for any reason, we have to continue to explain their needs and differences to others in a way that promotes understanding. At the beginning of each school year or new extracurricular activities, I discuss my child's wired differently condition with the provider or teacher. Also, I share a document that summarizes my daughter's likes, dislikes, and opportunities we are working on. It has made a tremendous difference to promote understanding and discuss environment modifications upfront.

However, try to find environments that are open to flexibility versus hardwired environments. It is important to be in environments that embody a growth mindset. You do not have the energy or time to be a martyr and bulldoze into each environment. It's not worth it for you, your child, or your family. Right now, your child needs you more than he/she needs you to transform the whole world. They do need you to transform their world. They need you to help make their world a better place.

It is worth noting that the world will typically see your child as an outlier and as a "square peg." There is a box. It may be a small box or a big box. The typical world mentality is to stay in the box or risk elimination. It is like teaching preschoolers to color inside of the line and if you color outside of the line, let's get rid of that stray line or that outlier. My advice is to start with an environment that has a bigger box of acceptance than typical places so that your square peg will have room to move and be protected.

Picking a box for your child is like baking a cake. Baking a cake is a science. By starting with the freshest ingredients, the right measurements, and the correct mixing, it is expected that the cake will turn out as planned. However, in baking a cake, if the stove is set to the wrong temperature, the cake may not rise as much as it could or be lopsided. It may not make a top bakery's standard but it wasn't the fault of the ingredients. That's how it is in a neurodiverse world. We want our children to be in environments that help them thrive and blossom in all ways that matter. We don't want our children to only rise some when they have the potential to rise more in a different environment. There are consequences if a child tries to fit into a harmful environment and compares themselves to others thriving in the same environment. It can leave our children feeling subpar and blaming themselves for not being accepted. The fault was that the environment was not suited to help our children succeed to their full ability.

By ensuring that an environment meets critical needs, it will help bring forth your child's purpose. Certain key traits are valuable for a special needs child. Does the environment:

- Believe in your child
- Commit to be there for your child
- Have gratitude for your child

The definition of an environment according to The Britannica Dictionary is "the conditions that surround someone or something: the conditions and influences that affect the growth, health, progress, etc., of someone or something."[26] An environment can be a doctor's office, a dentist's office, a preschool/daycare, a school, a church, your family home, or any extracurricular activities.

Before I understood some of the principles described in prior chapters, we were in the wrong environment. We were blindly throwing our child into an environment and "hoping" all would be well. It was like throwing our daughter into a den of wolves and expecting her to defend herself.

What is sending a child to a hostile environment doing to the child? It will cause trauma. So do not underestimate the importance of ensuring the right environment is set. Don't just send your child to an environment without evaluating it. We want our child to come out of an environment with self-esteem and confidence intact. We are not trying to do what everyone else wants or is doing. This is not the time to have a "throw a child in the deep end and trust they will learn to swim" mentality. Continue to see your child as a precious seed that needs a special combination of nutrients than other children. This is a special formula that you are learning and sharing with others.

Your child must have the right environment to thrive. Now that you know what your child needs, it is time to evaluate how well each environment meets your child's needs. Keep in mind, that what works for one child does not necessarily work for another child. Also, what may work for a child one time may not work at another time. Understanding the timing is very crucial.

The ultimate check is to observe how your child responds to the environment. Like a seed budding into a plant, is your child budding, or is your child wilting? If your child is experiencing excessive "meltdowns" or events, strongly evaluate if this is a stress indicator. Signs of stress in an environment include:

- Reluctance to go to school (or environment)
- Bursting into tears for small or no reason
- Becoming angry over small things
- Difficulty relaxing
- Frustrated when things do not go to plan

- Feeling threatened and responding with aggressive behaviors such as hitting, biting, or scratching
- Signs of anxiety and worry about activities or people in the environment
- Separation anxiety

LEARNING ENVIRONMENT

Let me give you a personal example. We had a situation where our five-year-old was having numerous meltdowns a week. At one point, the school was contacting us daily. It seemed to happen in times when she was in transition, such as, going from the classroom to lunch or going to the gym. The calls or notes included scratching kids, screaming matches, and overall challenging behavior in the classroom/learning setting. We realized that we needed to change her environment. Our child was wilting. She didn't tell us that she didn't want to go to school. How could she, as it was all she knew? She was, however, telling us via challenging behavior. The burden is not on the child, it is on us- the parents. We shifted to an environment where the environment was one of extreme love and care. It was an environment that was small and catered to each child. The teacher and owner taught with a fierceness that nothing was wrong with our child. Our child bloomed. It was a teaching environment that allowed risk-taking in a safe environment. The tantrums stopped. Her self-esteem and confidence grew.

In another incident, I was excited to have my youngest daughter attend a camp that her older sisters had attended in the past. It was a program that was focused on science, math, and reading enrichment. She was excited to go because she knew her sisters had gone. When the class went outside, there was a sidewalk beside a busy highway. My daughter didn't want to walk on the sidewalk to get to the next building. She wanted to run and go to the playground. When she thought of camp, she thought of playing. However, this was not a playing camp. Later in the day, she ran out of the classroom and the teachers had to run to catch her due to the busy highway. In the classroom, she had a major tantrum and the camp called me to come pick her up. Much later, my daughter explained that she was trying to find the playground. I learned that this environment wasn't the right environment for my daughter. We didn't evaluate the environment to see if they could accommodate her. Nor did we prepare our daughter for what to expect. At that time, I only knew about sensory. She was not able to sit still as the camp required. She also had misaligned expectations of what the experience would be, so the experience failed.

We then tried another camp and applied the new insight and explained to the camp that our daughter had sensory needs. I knew the camp worked with autistic and special needs kids in the past, so I was excited that this would be a good fit. Although we did not have an autistic diagnosis at the time, I knew that sensory needs were a close cousin. However, this camp did not have the right structure either for my daughter. When I went to pick up my daughter, I was filled with happy anticipation to hear about her day. Instead, I was greeted by a distressed counselor who asked me to pull out of the carpool line and to the side. My heart dropped when the camp director told me my daughter was not welcome back on day two of the camp. The camp director went further to say don't come back for a few years. I was devastated. She stated that my daughter was immature and not able to absorb the engineering concepts. That was partially true and my daughter was looking for more play! My daughter kept running away and hiding under the building at the camp. She said it was boring and she wanted to play. It was not the right environment for my daughter and I had to accept that, no matter the success my other daughters had with the program. I applied part of my learnings but hadn't learned to fully prep my daughter and assess the environments yet.

Learning environments can be in school or out of school. For example, our youngest daughter was in swim lessons in an environment that seemed great on the surface —small classes, ideal time, and receptive to developing our child. However, there was an insensitive teacher who impacted her progress. The teacher, while pushing her to another level in swim class, violated a trust point; my daughter thought she was drowning. Too early in the process, the teacher removed his support from under her back and let her sink without helping her. He also used rough language and an insensitive tone. This experience set her back in her swimming process by 6 months. She regressed in her swimming journey and was wary of the male teachers. After talking with other parents who observed the incident, I discovered this particular teacher had an unfortunate reputation. The business was supportive and released this teacher from teaching other students. They identified another swim teacher who was experienced with special needs students and this helped our daughter get back on track with learning how to swim.

Learning environments may be mixed, neurodiverse environments with neurotypical and neurodivergent kids. The environment must treat each student with the expectation they can be successful. Neurodivergent students may need modifications. All children can succeed with the right support. There is a shared partnership between you and the school. Ideally, this is a process of shepherding the release of the imprisoned splendor inside of your child through continuous learning and application. In his poem from Paracelsus, Robert Browning talks about the pure beauty that lies within us as hidden splendor.[27] Learning environments that serve our neurodivergent children should be vested in this discovery process.

EXTRACURRICULAR ENVIRONMENT

Extracurricular activities expose children to different environments and social activities. All children learn by doing and exposure. The key for differently wired children is which activities do you pursue for your child. Individual activities such as martial arts and swimming were good activities for our daughters. For our daughter who is autistic with sensory sensitivities, martial arts was a good activity up to a point. She didn't know the strength of her punch, and at five years old, was unable to articulate her feelings about being punched back. Another daughter hid in the bathroom when it was time for punching exercises due to her sensory challenges. Both would have a delayed reaction at times and would cry in the car leaving practice. We eventually stopped martial arts. Although it was a supportive environment, it wasn't the best fit for our girls because of the season we were in.

Swimming was an excellent activity for our girls. Once I learned that water could help with sensory integration, as well as a safety skill, we incorporated it as a part of our routine. The girls progressed to the point where they were going to swim meets. At one of our first big meets at a summer event, we had an experience where our youngest daughter did not want to get out of the pool without her flip-flops. She was sensitive to touch and feeling; how the floor surrounding the competition pool felt and looked mattered greatly to her. She was also concerned about dirtiness and germs. She swam fast and got to the end and refused to get out of the pool without her flip-flops to immediately put on her feet. When I realized what was happening, I rushed them over to her as I was working as a swim volunteer to be near her. I explained to her summer swim coach that she had sensory challenges and did not like the feel of the floor. In my mind, this was a small modification to make to help my daughter compete in swimming. She was fast and felt a newfound confidence from achieving in her meets. What was the choice? I could be embarrassed and pull her from the meet and further isolate her from others. Or I could pick the right battle and advocate for an accommodation to address what was bothering her. The coach warned me that I would need to work with desensitizing her as she would not be allowed this flexibility in more competitive meets. Fortunately, we were able to keep her swimming by assessing the environment and modifying where necessary.

VACATION ENVIRONMENT

Vacations are a time of bonding and exploring destinations for families. It can be stressful with any child but especially with special needs children. With planning and a supportive environment, it can be a wonderful adventure.

We decided to go to Disney World as a family vacation in 2019. Disney truly understands customer service and extends that understanding to the special needs and wired differently world. However, before we got to Disney, we needed to take our first plane ride as a family. From discussing with our daughter's social skills counselor, we needed to ensure the environment was right for them and they knew what to expect in the environment. Our social skills counselor highly recommended "frontloading" as a tool to help prepare for a successful vacation. Frontloading is when you prepare a child by removing the anxiousness of an experience. It involves walking through the scenarios and allowing them opportunities to experience the scenarios as much as possible before the event. Therefore, we watched videos on checking in at the airport, boarding the plane, and riding on the plane. We also role-played the events and answered any questions they had. We wanted our girls to know what to expect so that their anxiety was low. We also were able to sign up for special check-in processes that allowed us to avoid waiting in certain parts of the line and to be escorted through check-in. Waiting and uncertainty can be added stressors for children who experience sensory integration or autism.

We focused on travel preparation for our youngest, autistic daughter. However, all of our daughters benefited from this exercise. When we got to the airport, my daughters knew what to expect. Our middle daughter was still a little fearful on the plane because she thought that the plane would fall. The flexibility to sit with her dad comforted her.

At Disney, we found the customer experience team wearing blue shirts. Their role was to make sure we were able to get the full value out of our experience. Through preparation, we knew what we could ask for and how flexible to make our day to allow for periods of rest. It was so invaluable to have the flexibility to skip lines, schedule when your ride would be, and show up at a designated time for your ride or event.

We did not have any meltdowns and were able to enjoy the adventure through heavy planning and front loading. This methodology can be applied to other destinations to ensure your child can enjoy vacations on their terms.

FAMILY ENVIRONMENT

The family environment is the most important environment for your children as it will be the consistent element as they grow. As we learned the language and the words to understand our journey, my husband and I discovered that, once again, change began with us. We needed to rewire our family environment. For instance, I realized that our "go, go" household was not conducive to our children's brains. My husband and I grew up in a home where the kids were expected to align to what the adults said with no questions asked. Many times, we would shift our daughters from their activity without a warning. As we were on the go a lot, these shifts could be very emotional and stressful for all of us. It was revolutionary to give a thirty-minute heads-up to our child that a switch was pending. It looked a little like this — "We are going to the store in 30 minutes. You have 15 minutes to look at your show. Then, we need to turn off the television so that you can put your shoes on." Finally, after 30 minutes, we would say time to go and our child would follow us to the car. The key was giving advance notice.

We acquired many tools to incorporate into our home environment; from visual schedules and visual timers, to calm down corners and weighted blankets. One of my favorite tools is incorporating vision boards at the start of the school year to establish a vision and goals. It was a way for our daughters to document and share what they wanted to accomplish. With a little coaching, as they got older, they would cover a broad range of their lives from personal to school. We would celebrate their vision and encourage them as a family. As our daughters took action to accomplish the goals on their vision board, we would point those items out on their vision board, which was hanging in their rooms. The vision board became a guiding light and a tool to mark when to celebrate progress.

Once one of my daughters made a board that highlighted where she glowed and where she needed to grow. The glow items were reminders of the traits and skills she exhibited and did well. The grow items were the skills she was working on. It became a tool to highlight her progress toward her grow skills. The glow side celebrates her uniqueness and her accomplishments.

Doing exercises together as a family allows family bonding and is a fun way to practice sensory integration exercises. We would vary the exercises based on our schedule. For our family, exercise included walks on a trail, riding a bike, creating Stringfield Olympics, or going to the gym.

Establishing a safe and welcoming home environment may not always be easy; jealousy and misunderstandings can exist between siblings. With three girls, we definitely saw normal sibling rivalry on top of the special conditions that we needed to take into consideration. Sometimes we would see jealously related to one daughter sitting in a seat before the other did in our van. We eventually assigned seats for each daughter to stop the rivalry.

However, the home environment must always be undergirded with love no matter what. What a blessing to see children reciprocate what we share with them. When our oldest daughter perceived that my husband was having a challenging day at work, she wrote a note of encouragement to say, “You can do it, Daddy.” On our birthdays, our daughters work together to create a production of celebration from a collective of notes, homemade decorations, special songs, innovative meals, and creative poems. Your children will give what they see. We are not aiming for perfection but for progress.

There were a few times when our children were growing up that we needed a babysitter. Before bringing the babysitter into our home and trusting our daughters with them, we needed to evaluate how they would incorporate into our environment. As our children were growing up, we were very particular about who watched our daughters. This was for two main reasons. First, we knew our daughters were unique, although we didn't have any names or diagnoses for navigating. Second, we knew these adults were extensions of our family. We desired for the individuals to be people that our daughters had good experiences with already. Usually, our babysitter was a former teacher of one or more of the girls. Early on, we realized our daughters did not like newness. We would need to show them how it relates to something they had already experienced. To prepare the babysitter, I would discuss and leave a detailed list of our daughters' allergies, likes, and dislikes. It would also include calming strategies, routines, and tips. We would make this a comprehensive list to have a better chance for an uninterrupted night out.

Also, the family environment includes extended family. It is important to ensure that extended family gatherings and houses are conducive to your children's needs. Based on what you have learned are nonnegotiable standards, set boundaries. Do you need to limit time for events because your child needs a nap every day at the same time? Will your child be unable to take a nap unless certain conditions are met? Are you able to frontload your child with expectations of who will be at an event, or how long you will be at an event? Limit overwhelm by reducing unpredictability as much as possible.

Family members can also shame children based on their childhood experiences and expectations. Be careful of words that may cause harm for your child such as "act your age" or "you are too big for that." Confront the damaging behavior for the sake of your child. You may need to limit your child's exposure to certain family members.

MEDICAL ENVIRONMENT

Your child must be seen by medical personnel who are aware of neurodiversity. It is a must to have a doctor who listens and does not discount symptoms or behaviors. We once had an appointment with an acclaimed research psychiatrist and ADHD specialist. We traveled an hour, one way, to meet the doctor. When I described our ADHD journey and medicines, the doctor discounted the prior negative reaction to the medication. In addition, the doctor seemed to rush through the appointment and was more focused on the payment. I left feeling not understood or heard and rushed.

In a medical environment, you want a professional who listens and is sensitive and caring. You do not want to introduce trauma by being in an environment that doesn't see your child. Seeing includes deeply listening to your child's feelings, your concerns, and being invested in focusing on your child's splendor. This also includes being aware of and embracing cultural differences. As an example, many times autistic Black children are less likely to get the medical interventions and support they need due to the lack of system design for Black parents.[28] Research shows healthcare access issues, healthcare communication, or prohibitive costs for treatment adds complexity for autism diagnosis for Black and Hispanic children. Transparent and inclusive dialogue between parents and doctors is key. Parents may not have the information to push doctors and doctors may not take symptoms as serious for Black and Hispanic communities.

WORSHIP ENVIRONMENT

The faith environment is a key element in many families. However, it is still an environment to be evaluated and accommodated for your child. We are regular church attendees. By observing our daughter, we learned that the loud, concert-like music would bother her. We would modify our behavior by sitting at the back of the sanctuary where the sound was a little less. Sometimes we would arrive after that point in the service. Later, we learned to add noise-canceling headphones for our daughter in the mix. My daughters also had difficulty sitting in the service the whole time. So we sat further back in the sanctuary, where she could sit on the floor, versus the chair, without bothering anyone else in the service. We needed flexibility as we learned to worship a little differently and continue to be a part of the service. We needed our child to be able to make noise and move around without criticism. We also shared our children's preferences and needs with the children's group ministers. There were a few incidents of meltdowns that we navigated over the years. Fortunately, our church was able to adjust with us and allow our children's faith to grow.

CHECKLIST

How do you evaluate an environment? This is the checklist I use to assess if this is an environment that works for our children. Does the environment show love in how it serves you and your child? Use the **LOVE** acronym. Does the environment have **LOVE**?

> **L — level up capability** — Level up capability is the potential to increase the greatness of your whole

child. The whole child includes your child's spirit, soul, and body. Your child's soul is made up of their mind, will, emotions, intellect, and imagination. If the environment isn't helping your child to level up across these areas, it is potentially hurting your child and causing trauma. Trauma to your child's spirit, soul, or body may take time to recover from. Does the environment show the capability for your child's intellect to grow? Does the environment strengthen your child's body through healthy foods and exercise? Will the emotional support provided help your child to blossom?

O — order — Order is the way things are arranged or done. Neurodivergent children need structure. Structure gives predictability that provides comfort. Order can be provided by visual charts, visual clocks, and consistency in time or activities. Does it seem like the environment has some level of consistency and order? Or is the environment more random with no way to set any expectations for the child? Although order is needed, this is not a call for rigidity but a comforting expectation setting.

V — vulnerability — Vulnerability is the capability to grow together through uncertainty with flexibility. Do you see elements of flexibility and change built into the environment? Or is it a more rigid environment? Your child will not grow if the box is drawn and the rules are set with no flexibility to change or at least move the box. If it is a rigid environment, you could be expelled quickly anyway, due to a "you are canceled" or "our way, or no way" attitude. Is this environment willing to provide consistent communication with you and demonstrate respect for your journey together as a team to support your child? Are they willing to ask for input and feedback? Are they willing to change and offer accommodations based on the needs of your child?

E — empathy — Empathy is the ability to see and share the feelings of others. Does this environment see you enough to walk in your shoes? Can the environment see through the eyes of the child, or is the environment forcing the child to see only through the eyes of the adult? Is the environment kind? Does the environment make you and your child feel welcome? A trusting environment will build you and your child up for empowerment. Does this environment see you and your child and provide genuine care? Or are you being stereotyped? Is your child ignored when they are considered to be misbehaving? Can the child see someone culturally like them in the environment? The child needs to be able to identify with other children in the environment of the same gender, race, and age if possible. Is it a neurodiverse environment? Relating to identity is a foundational block of empathy.

By using this acronym, it provides a proven framework for evaluating an environment and what you can expect from it. Then, you can create a strategy and plan for how you integrate yourself and your child into the environment. You will also have a better awareness of how much you can influence the environment and what areas need influencing. You will never know all until you are in an environment, but you will have a better idea. Gather your information for evaluation by visiting the environment first via in-person tours i.e., school tours. This will give you a view of the culture. Sometimes an in-person preview visit is not feasible, i.e going to Disney before the Disney trip. However, you can view pictures on websites or social media like YouTube. Some businesses may even have online tours.

Next, talk to people who are already in the environment or have been in the environment. This is the time to use your tribe for discovery. Other special needs parents will be happy to share their positive or negative experiences in social media groups or directly one on one. You can also ask others for recommendations and compare. Perhaps, you can ask for examples and details based on your specific needs. If your child needs extra bathroom time, this is a group that will understand and provides specific feedback based on their experience.

Armed with information and feedback, you can then weigh the pros and cons to make a decision. After evaluating the environment, it may be obvious that a certain environment is not the right fit for your child. If you are unsure, you can do a trial with the targeted environment as applicable. For example, when choosing a school, it is ideal for you to see your child operate in the environment, for the ultimate test, for a short time. Then, you can do a reevaluation of your assessment — was it on track, and does the environment work for your child?

In some cases, you may add an environment to supplement the community of environments for your child. For example, in addition to swimming, we knew our daughter needed more social engagement. So, we added Girls Scouts for a short time as well as Girls on the Run for social exposure.

In summary, our children are our seeds in a garden. Their environment is important as they will absorb what is in their environment. It is important to evaluate each environment with L.O.V.E. Your child is precious cargo that you are protecting. Your child is worthy of love.

GROWTH KEYS: REWIRE YOUR ENVIRONMENT

1. Evaluate all environments including your home with L.O.V.E.
2. Plant your child where they will grow.
3. Pay attention to all feedback from your child.

Inspiring Quotes

When a flower doesn't bloom, you fix the environment in which it grows, not the flower. — Alexander Den Heijer

You get the best effort from others not by lighting a fire beneath them, but by building a fire within. — Bob Nelson

Without dreams and goals there is no living, only merely existing, and that is not why we are here. — Mark Twain

Autistics are the ultimate square pegs. And the problem with pounding a square peg into a round hole is not that the hammering is hard work. It's that you're destroying the peg. — Paul Collins

Allowing a student with a hidden disability (High-Functional Autism, ADHD, Anxiety, Dyslexia, Tourette's) to struggle academically or socially when all that is needed for success are appropriate accommodations and explicit instruction, is no different than failing to provide a ramp for a person in a wheelchair. — Joe Becigneul

Children learn more from what you are than what you teach. — W. E. B. DuBois

To measure the success of our societies, we should examine how well those with different abilities, including persons with autism, are integrated as full and valued members. — Ban Ki-moon

Every child deserves a champion — an adult who will never give up on them, who understands the power of connection and insists that they become the best they can possibly be. — Rita Pierson

Love cures people — both the ones who give it and the ones who receive it. — Karl A. Menninger

Reflecting Questions

- Which environments should be reevaluated for serving your child?
- Which environments are serving your child well? Why?
- What key factors have your child been missing in their environments?

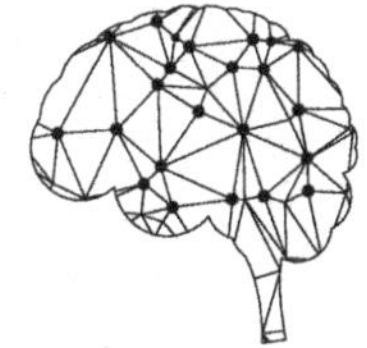

CHAPTER 7

In electrical engineering, a bridge circuit is known as a circuit to convert an electric current from an unknown to a known, direct polarity. It is like a shortcut to get to the desired result. In this chapter, we focus on seven building blocks that will help accelerate rewired outcomes.

ONE TEAM

The adult support of the special needs child must be one team. If there are two parents in the home, you must be unified. No matter what each parent's expectations about the family structure were, it is important to grow together and create new expectations. As one, share knowledge and compare notes. If it is possible, attend IEP and teacher meetings together as a team. Inevitably, one person will hear one thing slightly different and you two can share and adjust later as a team. If there are separate households, there will be extra steps necessary to ensure clear communication and alignment through the parenting journey for the sake of the child. A one-team approach includes extended family members such as grandparents, aunts, or uncles who play a significant role in raising a special needs child. They will all need to act as one team.

TAP OUT

There are times when you are empty and beyond your energy reserve level. The key is to try not to reach that level if possible before asking for help. Know yourself and when you need to tap out. My grandfather used to like to watch wrestling. In team wrestling, there is a time when your partner can tap out and tap you in when they need a break. Use the same concept with parenting. Tap out to hand off to the other parent or a trusted friend.

I recognize that not everyone is blessed with a loving spouse who is willing to learn and embrace a rewired parenting mindset. It is a privilege to have two parents in the home. We were able to tap out as needed for a mental break. As a single parent, you may not have an opportunity to tap out when you are trying to go to work. However, establish trusted relationships that can support you and create an opportunity to "tap out" at key moments for you to re-energize.

The gym became a way I could tap out since it provided quality childcare. I would sign in my daughters and go to an exercise class or take a quick swim. The individual attention and small environment accommodated our undiagnosed special needs kids quite well. I was able to participate in self-care by relieving stress and staying healthy.

STAY CURIOUS

As a parent, you may not always get it perfect and it may not always be easy. There will be an ebb and flow. Rest in this journey. Watch for your child evolving through the process age by age, grade by grade, and year by year. A tool that worked early in the journey may need to shift to another tool as your child gets older. You may wonder if it is puberty, autism, or some other neurodiverse characteristic. Or is the challenge normal sibling rivalry? The key is to remain curious, as explored in the previous chapters. Be flexible as you parent your child.

TRIAL AND ERROR

This journey will take time and patience with wired differently children. There will be times when it looks like you made a decision that delayed a result. Have compassion for yourself. There will be times of trial and error. Your intent is good for your child's success. After speaking with a colleague, I learned that social skills training is a positive intervention step. We tried three social skills groups before we got to the right one for my daughter. However, I saw the benefit and gained knowledge for myself and my daughter in each one. The first social skills group was play-based. I learned new terminology regarding big feelings, which are especially hard to navigate for neurodiverse children. In the second social skills group, I learned to stand up for what wasn't working for my daughter. In the third social group, I found a community that understood our needs and was vested to help us be great.

Now, we have our daughters begging for social skills sessions because they know it helps them. In this community of respect, they know they are seen.

Move forward in your rewired parenting journey. You don't need to be rescued. The journey will teach you more than you know about life and yourself.

RELEASE GUILT AND SHAME

As my husband and I navigated challenging situations involving our daughters, there were times when we felt guilty. I remember a particular time when I went to pick up my daughter from preschool, the administrator stopped me before I went to her classroom and asked for me to step into her office. She told me that my daughter had a tough day. The teacher informed the administrator that my daughter had pushed the teacher in the stomach. The administrator was concerned as the teacher had recently had abdominal surgery. She started to ask me a series of questions in rapid fire. Is there something going on in the home that would cause this aggressive behavior? Are you going through a divorce? Is there fighting in the home? Anything we should know about? I said no and I was swimming in shame and, for some reason, guilt. I didn't know what to say and couldn't address the comment that my daughter pushed the teacher. After only a week of enrollment, we were soon expelled from that school.

Did something abnormal happen during the pregnancy? That question was one of many on the medical history questionnaire we completed. That one question started days of searching and reliving the pregnancy. What did I eat? Did I work too hard? Not enough water? Did I cause this?

None of those behavior and thought patterns served me or our daughters well. This perspective and battle came after ridding myself of feelings of inadequacy and understanding that I had no reason to feel guilty or shame. It was time to know my child and apply that knowledge to discover the best environments and support for her.

DROP THE MASK

Drop the mask in front of your child. It is okay to model that as parents, we can have big feelings too. It is an opportunity to be authentic, heal together, and learn together. Don't try to hold it together. Don't hide your feelings and bury them in front of your kids. Be where you are — angry, sad, frustrated but do no harm. Don't destroy relationships or build walls with your feelings. These feelings don't describe who you are. Live with your whole heart — physical and spiritual —> (soul) mind, will, intellect, imagination.

It is ok to share with your child:
"I made a mistake."
"I'm sorry."
"I need a moment to pause and take a breath."
"I can't talk about this now."
"I don't know what to do right now."

Share with others as it can help others. As humans, we tend to hide the hard areas. Look at social media. Most people post about the easy or happy times versus the struggles. That toxic positivity can leave others feeling alone and like a failure. Sharing your experience as a special needs parent, in person or via social media, can help other parents.

REPEAT THE PROCESS

If you have multiple children, there is a delicate balance required to ensure you are meeting the needs of all of your children. It can be overwhelming — take it one step, one diagnosis at a time. Gain information about each diagnosis though leveraging resources --books, podcasts, and seminars. Spend quality time with each child, even five minutes dedicated to one child matters.

RECOMMENDED BOOKS AND RESOURCES

Overcoming Dyslexia by Sally Shaywitz, M.D.
The Dyslexic Advantage by Brock L. Eide, M.D., M.A. and Fernette F. Eide, M.D.
Brain-Body Parenting by Mona Delahooke, PhD.
ADDitude - www.additudemag.com

GROWTH KEYS: TIPS FOR PARENTS

1. Be unified as a parenting team.
2. Free yourself and the rest will follow.
3. Learn with your child.

Inspiring Quotes

It's impossible to judge others, once you stop judging yourself. — Tiffany Dufu

No one gets a great life wishing for it. — Joyce Meyer

Kids don't remember what you try to teach them. They remember what you are. — Jim Henson

In all kinds of ways — if we are willing, our children take us into places in our hearts we didn't know existed. — Dr. Shefili Tsabary

Behind every young child who believes in himself is a parent who believed first. — Matthew Jacobson

There is no such thing as a perfect parent. So just be a real one. — Sue Atkins

There is no greater leadership challenge than parenting. — Jim Rohn

Don't wish it was easier, wish you were better. Don't wish for less problems, wish for more skills. Don't wish for less challenges, wish for more wisdom. — Jim Rohn

Reflecting Questions

- ➢ What challenging situations have you experienced as a family?
- ➢ Who do you need to add to your tap out circle?
- ➢ What areas are you committing to drop the mask and share?

CHAPTER 8

Your child has been diagnosed. What do you do now? What now for you and your family? There were so many thoughts and emotions at the beginning of our journey. Now, we see the progress through the perseverance of applying a rewired parenting mindset.

When my daughter was initially diagnosed with dyslexia, dysgraphia, and ADHD, we did not understand either one of those medical conditions. I felt conflicting emotions from sadness to anger to fear. Our daughter was in the third grade, reading on a first-grade level. How did I not know this before? Her psychologist said we had been working extremely hard by providing private occupational therapy, speech therapy, and swimming lessons in advance of an official diagnosis. The good news was that the support mechanisms were helpful. The psychologist shared that perhaps now with the diagnosis we could target some of the therapy accordingly. We were able to drop the occupational therapy and tune the speech therapy to focus on reading support. I started to read and research dyslexia so I could explain the diagnosis to my daughter. It all felt so overwhelming. At the same time, we had two other daughters who very much needed us too. Our youngest was getting settled in public school and we were navigating how to help her adjust in school. So, we focused on addressing dyslexia with my middle daughter and ignoring dysgraphia and ADHD for the moment. We would later discover that we would need to revisit this decision when we did not see the progress we expected. We started with a 504 Plan to assist at school with dyslexia. A 504 Plan protects the rights of kids with disabilities in US schools and is covered under Section 504 of the Rehabilitation Act of 1973. The 504 Plan is a formal plan that schools develop to give children with disabilities the support they need.

Further research suggested my daughter would benefit from Ortho-Gillingham (OG) teaching methodology. This method would teach the way my daughter would learn best with her dyslexic wiring. I asked the school about the OG teaching style and the intervention teacher did not seem to know what OG was. I proceeded to buy an OG workbook and reviewed the lessons with my daughter each week. I soon realized this was not my gift to teach my daughter with the workbook and sought a teacher or tutor to help. We found and hired a Wilson-certified teacher to support my daughter through the school year. Wilson is a structured literacy program based on OG principles. We saw a little improvement. We also started the process to move from a 504 Plan to an IEP. We hired an advocate to help us with ensuring we had the right accommodations based on the doctor's recommendations for our daughter as well as her needs. As covered in Chapter 5, the advocate was a great help since we did not know what to ask for or understand the process.

By talking with other parents who were on a similar dyslexic journey, I discovered that we needed to consider seeing our pediatrician to treat the ADHD in parallel. I learned that treating ADHD plays a role in allowing the right level of focus to acquire a different and new skill like reading. Based on research, we decided to try a high dosage level of fish oil with a healthy diet to complement any medication we may try. We noticed some improvements in sensory impacts. Then our pediatrician used genetic testing to help determine how a particular medicine may interact with my daughter's body. Even with this help, we had an adverse experience with the first ADHD medication we tried. However, we did eventually see progress that helped my daughter and allowed her to absorb more knowledge in school.

During the summer, we hired a teacher to work with her daily and used a home-based Ortho-Gillingham program to assist along with Wilson-based tutoring on the weekend. It changed the game. Our daughter entered 4th grade reading close to 4th-grade level!

Not only did she start reading the menu at restaurants as mentioned in chapter 4, she was also reading the descriptions to pick the family movie. No longer was she picking a movie by looking at the picture only. She was reading the description by herself. She was also reading the signs as we drove down the highway. She was reading more and also learning how to use assistive technology to help her with longer assignments.

We went through the same process for our youngest daughter once we recognized some ADHD symptoms we saw in our middle daughter in our youngest daughter. We started the official identification process for her with the same private psychologist we used before. The psychologist confirmed the ADHD diagnosis, but also saw symptoms that were reflected in autism and encouraged us to see an autism specialist. I was floored but relieved when we learn about our daughter's autism diagnosis. The same process we went through for our dyslexic daughter we needed to go through now.

Unfortunately, life doesn't stop. We both worked full-time, demanding jobs. We weren't able to do this all serially, but we needed to operate simultaneously to address our daughters' needs. It was very hard. You may find yourself in a similar situation. Here are a few top recommendations for strength as you go through this experience:

THE TRIBE

You need your Tribe! A tribe is a similar group of parents who are in the boat with you and navigating the journey on their terms. These individuals will share resources and ideas with you. They will remind you that although you feel alone, you are not alone.

When I was experiencing labor pains during pregnancy, I closed my eyes. During this time, I began to visualize that I was floating on a gentle moving boat rising and falling on the waves of contractions. This image in my mind alone gave me peace. The transformational moment was when I saw other women standing on the shore. These women were smiling and welcoming me to the other side. They were mothers and had gone through this journey. If they could do this, I could do this. It was possible for me to make it regardless of how I felt. This visualization calmed me and inspired me!

Therefore, it is important to find your tribe to inspire you during the wired differently journey. Having a tribe will keep you strong and allow you to be comfortable challenging yourself to be resourceful. A tribe allows you a safe place to cry, to be vulnerable, and to say

I don't know. This place will help to free you from shame. These are your peeps! These are those that are in the no judgment zone. It is a place of empathy. As Brene Brown states, "shame cannot stay where empathy is." This is your lifeline to help you navigate this journey. The place that will allow you to be comfortable being uncomfortable. A place to allow you to throw open the door to your house and allow them to peep in your corners.

For us, it was first finding our tribe through social media groups and online communities. Initially, I was a silent participant in reading the discussion threads. By reading the threads, I was able to find comfort in the similarity of my thoughts being echoed in what was being posted. The words were giving me validation that I was on a similar journey and my feelings were not alone. Some of the parents were asking about picky eaters, where to find resources, and how to deal with challenging behaviors. I was home.

This is a tribe that will add to your greenhouse environment for your seed; allowing you to know what is available for your seed. Then you can start to help others. Helping others will also help you build strength for your journey. It helped me to feel the love of this community.

Podcasts can be helpful to validate your feelings and give you new tools. Some may be local to you and others may be international. I took classes and seminars with educators and other parents. Local universities may have certification workshops and a library of resources available to you. This was so helpful.

Expanding your view will shift your perspective. You are part of a complete ecosystem, navigating neurodiversity and special needs parenting. You are not alone.

It took reaching a breaking point with an autism diagnosis, work, and life, to try therapy for myself for the first time. In the Black community, therapy can still be stigmatized. I broke this bondage for myself and my family and learned the power of therapy. I connected with a therapist/counselor who was familiar with special needs as well as helping parents. This is a unique situation and you can't get through this by yourself. Professionals who had been through this and guided other parents through it are very valuable. This was a safe place to discuss my pain, my frustration, and other feelings.

I also counted as part of our tribe our cleaning company. Having a cleaning service come through twice a month, freed our time and sanity. My husband added lawn care to include grass cutting and bush maintenance to our tribe. We were balancing transportation to multiple swim practices, multiple schools, doctor appointments, and support services. We saw swim practice as a part of therapy. It was so helpful for social skills, sensory integration, and an important life skill. During these times we use these transportation moments to encourage and teach our daughters, but it didn't leave much time to take care of some of the basics. We also leveraged grocery delivery and online shopping regularly. It was a necessity.

REJUVENATE

Through this journey, we forget how much we are doing as parents. We are wearing all of these hats. Sometimes you will get tired. It is an opportunity to listen to your body and mind and note that you need to rest for a moment. We must rejuvenate ourselves through whole body exercise. I suggest:

1. Mind Resilience Exercises
2. Modeling Boundaries Exercises
3. Movement Exercises

Mind resilience exercises strengthen your mind by clearing it and refocusing on your values. I loved to do what I call a gratitude walk. This is where I would walk in nature and observe the trees, and the birds, and enjoy the breeze. During this time, I would say a prayer or just be thankful for that moment. Then I would listen to an inspirational or motivational book during the rest of my walk. Afterward, I would feel so inspired and have additional clarity to face the challenges of the day.

There will be times when you will be overwhelmed. You will need to ensure you are creating boundaries for yourself to pause and breathe. Do not continue to push yourself. If you have strong feelings yourself — name them— and say what you are going to do. It is good for you as well as serves as modeling for your child. Drop the mask by saying, "Kids, I am feeling overwhelmed and I'm going outside for 10 minutes." Rejuvenation may also mean taking a mental health day from work or extra rest time on the weekend. Refill your spirit and soul with the good things. I like to walk the beach and observe the birds flying over the ocean. At times, it feels like my very soul is being refreshed with each breath I take standing on the beach.

Movement exercises are key. Sometimes stress can get stuck in your body and exercises can elicit an emotional release. I would exercise sometimes and be overwhelmed with emotions. I would start to cry for no reason. This was another sign that I had pushed myself too hard without refilling.

During trying times, I found a haven at the gym. I would go to a Synergy (Zumba+dance) class while my daughter was at swim practice, at least twice a week. I remember in one class the song "Glorious" by Macklemore was playing. I had never heard this song before and it reflected my experience in Synergy class. First, you must know that I am a clumsy dancer. Second, the dance class was done with the main lights off and only included dance club dim lighting. Third, it was mainly women in the class. This equated to freedom! The darkness of the class provided an illusion of hiding my clumsy imperfections until I got to the place to comfortably be me. We were free to celebrate each other. It was a moment filled with tangible joy. Laughing at myself, I could keep moving even through my mistakes. It felt like this mirrored my feelings about my parenting journey. In this class, we had these empowering feelings of "we got this" and "we are in it to succeed together." This was part of my community and tribe. The song exclaims,

> "I feel glorious, glorious
> Got a chance to start again
> I was born for this, born for this
> It's who I am, how could I forget?
> I made it through the darkest part of the night
> And now I see the sunrise
> Now I feel glorious, glorious
> I feel glorious, glorious"

It's not over. It will be hard. "Do it hard," as Les Brown says. You are resilient. You are enough. God is enough. Your tribe is (will be) enough. You can't serve your child well from an empty place. This is about filling you, so you give from a full space.

LESSONS LEARNED

Remember to embrace this journey. When you get a little further down the road, you will begin to appreciate what you are learning in this process about yourself and life. The ultimate learning is that the rewiring starts with you! Hence the name of this book — Rewired Parenting.

Below are my top twelve lessons that I treasure and see as impacting every aspect of my life.

1. **Protect My "It's Possible" Mindset.** No matter what I feel or see in the natural, I must keep a belief that joy and happiness is possible. Winning is also possible as long as I have the right mindset and don't give up. This includes a belief that if I can see it and believe it is possible for me, I can have it. This leads me to seeking, dreaming, visualizing, moving, and being. It starts the process of letting go of shame and fear! Have Faith! Be resilient. My journey may not look like everyone else's and I am okay with that.
2. **The Process is Important.** There are no shortcuts, embrace the process in everything I do. Just like my daughter had to go through the process of learning differently with dyslexia, I must be willing to see the process through to the end. Patience is a necessary skill to grow.
3. **Celebrate All Wins.** It may seem small to others but I must celebrate each day to build confidence to keep moving. Not moving is paralysis and death. During my day, I celebrate every task accomplished. This extends to celebrating my team, coworkers, and family members.
4. **Create a Culture of Gratitude.** In everything I do, I find opportunities to give thanks. By being thankful, I will identify goodness. I rewire myself to find good versus focusing on the challenges. It becomes a culture of gratitude that promotes satisfaction and appreciation. It is like a feedback loop that allows

feeling and giving of gratitude continually. The spotlight is no longer on what I don't have but focus on the goodness of what I do have. Again as Dr. Tal Ben-Shahar states "when you appreciate the good, the good appreciates." Lean into joy!

5. **Be Brave! Be ME!** Observing my child, my unapologetically, unique child, inspired me to do the same in my life. My journey with my children has changed my approach to how I show up in my life. I show up with bravery. I am living a fuller life in my career, for my family, and for me. I say if I like something or if I don't like something — out loud! Be free!
6. **Drop Burdens by Setting Boundaries!** I do not need an excuse for self-care or to do something for myself. I do not need to worry about how others perceive me. I used to feel like I would have to justify my no. Just saying, "No, this doesn't work for me "is enough.
7. **The Power of Community.** Being with like-minded individuals is powerful. Watching my daughters struggle and thrive and watching them expand is powerful. I know it is important to connect with a community that can help you thrive.
8. **The Power of Now.** Be present in the moment. Make each moment matter. See each moment as a gift. Tie this to #4 by looking for the good in each moment. Take action! These moments that matter will build and create a protective, insulating joy.
9. **Don't Assume Ill Intent.** I now have a different view of diversity as I build teams and operate within organizations. I think through inclusion and how we can represent multiple voices to reach our greatest impact. It is a proven fact that diverse teams lead to innovation. So, I ponder thoughts such as — "What does an IEP look like for an employee who may

be on my team?" or "What accommodations should I or the environment make to allow them to reach their greatness?" At all costs, I assume positive intent no matter what I see. If we assume ill intent, we typically launch into an exercise to fix someone or the situation. The sum total of our knowledge will never compare to what we do not know. Our understanding of others' perspectives will always be limited. If we see the potential of greatness in others and never limit it to our definition of greatness, we are orienting from a positive point of view. Our power lies in our ability to embrace others' uniqueness and let go of the need to control scenarios. This belief also expands into how to approach if someone says a statement or takes an action that may be controversial. In the words of the 7 Habits by Stephen Covey, this learning is like the "seek first to understand" habit. In fact, at work, a co-worker mistook what I said when I asked for a positive person to be sent as a delegate to a meeting. The co-worker sharply told me that she is always positive. Our brands and relationship of trust prompted us to seek to understand. From her cultural perspective, my comment was offensive, and doubted her capabilities. From my perspective, I was communicating that an upbeat ambassador was important for the meeting. To reconcile our communication styles, we had to start with not assuming ill intent and seeking to understand.

10. **Work The Tools.** I have a new love for weighted blankets and comfort blankets! I sit at my desk with a weighted blanket on my lap at work. I also sleep with a heavy blanket each night. If I am a passenger on a long car trip, I need a blanket! This is a journey of self-discovery. I also love the power of taking a pause and an extra-long breath. When you see the

tools working for your children, don't be afraid to use them for yourself. In the bigger picture, you can't overanalyze. You must take action. Kids don't stop growing and exploring. It helps you see that you can't ignore the important stuff. At the end of the day, taking action keeps you moving and growing. Some actions may show immediate impact and others may be delayed. Don't stop. Keep taking steps.

11. **Know Thyself.** I know myself better and how factors such as rest are important for me to be successful. I know I get overwhelmed at dinner parties after a long day and need time to rejuvenate. Using strategy, I will create an exit plan if needed. No longer do I force myself to keep going and forget I was in a set of meetings that may have drained me. You can't serve from an empty cup. It is important to respect your personal boundaries and not give more than you have to give. Instead of tantrums, there may be other health-related consequences as an adult.
12. **Be Kind to Yourself**. I am my first friend. If I find myself being extremely critical of myself or my progress, I take a step back and ask, "What would I say to my friend?" It is important to be kind and patient with myself.

RECOMMENDED BOOKS

The Energy Bus by Jon Gordon
The Power of TED by David Emerald
QBQ! The Question Behind the Question by John G. Miller
Outliers by Malcolm Gladwell
Daring Greatly by Brene Brown

GROWTH KEYS: STRENGTH FOR THE JOURNEY

1. Embrace your tribe.
2. Fill your cup.
3. Embrace the learnings of the journey.

Inspiring Quotes

The first person I should try to change is me. — John C. Maxwell

All you can change is yourself, but sometimes that changes everything. — Gary W. Goldstein

I am just as worthy as anyone else and my actions will prove it. — Hal Elrod

Being a mother is learning about the strengths you didn't know you had, and dealing with fears you didn't know existed. — Linda Wooten

Never allow someone to be your priority while allowing yourself to be their option. — Mark Twain

Great leaders don't succeed because they are great. They succeed because they bring out the greatness in others. - Jon Gordon

Reflecting Questions

- What are you learning from your child on this journey?
- Who are important members of your tribe?

REWIRED FAITH

CHAPTER 9

Faith was and is important in this journey of parenting. God speaks in the quietest moments at times and in the smallest steps. Sometimes we could only see the next step forward and were unsure of what would come next. Sometimes, we felt like we were in complete darkness and unsure if we were looking up or down. However, we believed by faith that our daughters were not a burden, but a unique gift from God. We believed by faith that we would be a happy family no matter what. Faith is one of the nine segments of the Fruit of the Spirit declared in Galatians 5:22. The other eight include love, joy, peace, long-suffering, gentleness, goodness, meekness, and temperance. We believed all of these characteristics of the Spirit were at work in our life and would help us carry on, regardless of what our journey appeared to be. This was not our initial position. This is a position we came to after rewiring our faith to understand God's purpose is always at work even if we do not understand His purpose.

When going to a theme park, the ride and the anticipation of enjoying the ride is the focus of attention. However, if the line is extremely long, the wait in the line becomes the focus versus the ride. At Disneyland, the design engineers (Imagineers) reimagined the line from a straight one to a line that switches back and forth to allow people to interact with each other while waiting. The engineers also added artifacts to make the line a part of the ride experience instead of a separate activity. The attendees' line of sight is restricted to a few feet in front of them at all times so that the journey to the main event does not seem laborious. The Imagineers knew that how they framed the situation was key. Instead of focusing only on short-term gains of how to move the guests efficiently, the Imagineers focused on how to make the guests happier by improving the experience of the journey. They saw the journey from the eyes of their guests. The Imagineers focused on keeping expectations high for the overall experience moment by moment. They intentionally created a moment that mattered from beginning to end.

This example reminds me of the journey of walking this life with our children. It is important to see through the eyes of our children how they experience the journey of life moment by moment. Then, more importantly, to see through the eyes of God. As parents, we have to cultivate our expectations through this journey. God has high expectations and a different picture of what we see with our natural eyes. God has an "expected end" for us as the Bible says in Jeremiah 29:11. God has "plans to prosper" us and to give us "hope and a future." We are not alone. God is with us as we navigate what feels like "trouble." In Psalms 91:15, it says God is with me "in trouble" and will "deliver and honor" me. As we walked our journey and cultivated our expectations, deliverance appeared in the form of people with knowledge and wisdom for a certain piece of our journey. These were answers to our prayers. These were milestone moments that indicated we were not alone.

In my prayer time, during our parenting journey, God showed me a picture of the yellow brick road as in the book, *The Wizard of Oz,* by Frank L. Baum. There were challenging times in the book when the road was in disarray. Although Dorothy knew to stay on the yellow brick road to get to her destination, it was not clear which way to go to stay on the path. As Dorothy traveled, she sometimes needed to take a step and look around for the next step. As she moved, the next portion of the path was revealed. If she stayed still, she would not have made it to her goal. To apply this illustration to our parenting journey, God is with us and will reveal to us the next brick in our path. We can't stay distracted or discouraged by what we see. We can't stay paralyzed by the weight of the burden of being lost. We must trust God — step by step. You may only see one step to take, but when you trust God and take that step, the next step will appear. Be patient, and listen for God's direction. God is with you in your journey. He loves us so much as it says in I Corinthians 2:9, it has not entered into our hearts "the things God hath prepared or them that love him." It goes on in verse 10 to say that it will be revealed "unto us by his Spirit."

My husband and I believe God. The Holy Spirit is working with us and through us on this journey. The Holy Spirit will reveal to us His preparation for us and inspire our higher expectations for our family. By staying connected to God's heart, we will see the evidence of the Fruit of the Spirit for our children and family. At a particular moment, we may not understand where we are in the journey or how much more we have to overcome. However, we rested in God through His grace and a settled attitude that we are ok. We had an attitude that by keeping our mind on God and resting like a "tree planted by the rivers of water" we will prosper and succeed as it says in Psalms 1:2-3. Our appointed place is success no matter what. There was no longer a need to be in a heightened state of fear, anxiety, or frustration. When God so fully extends grace to us, we can also give grace to others with a settled attitude. We defined this new state as gratitude. When we can rest in gratitude, there is a peace that passes all understanding like it is stated in Philippians 4:7. My husband and I saw gratitude as an equation:

Grace + Attitude = Gratitude

This gratitude allowed us to be in a state of thankfulness. The more thankfulness we demonstrated; the more we had to be thankful. God multiplied our gratitude.

This doesn't mean we ignored the challenges we were facing. When the school called to discuss a bad day for our child, we were not feeling happy or having the best thoughts. However, we were able to have a perspective through gratitude that allowed us to pivot our mindset and faith. We were able to be grateful for each moment and look forward to the next moment with resiliency.

As an example, a behavioral incident happened in the school cafeteria with other children in my daughter's class. The kids were joking about inappropriate content. Through investigation, the school identified that although my daughter wasn't involved with the cafeteria incident, she was exposed to negative peer influences and inappropriate content outside of school hours. The incident prompted the school to notify me about the situation and her exposure. I was thankful that the incident happened so that we could address the negative friendships but also the technology boundaries we had in our home. My autistic daughter, who had struggled to make friends, was making a few friends. Unfortunately, some of these friends were focused on areas that my daughter had not been exposed to. Our daughter was learning, but not quite mastered, to discern if a friend was a good one or not. Just four months prior, she was crying that she did not have friends and was not sure who to invite to a party. Partnering friendship challenges with new technology freedoms, was an opportunity for negative exposure. Instead of being upset with the call, I saw the blessing in the call. I was thankful that we were given an opportunity to address this now while the exposure was a small seed.

Other times, if a school called to share behavior concerns, terms were used like aggression to describe her behavior. I remained in a state of curiosity and explored, through principles discussed earlier in this book, if this school was the right environment for my daughter. I was grateful that I was able to have additional data points, coupled with God's direction for analyzing the environment. This was an opportunity for me to ensure my daughter experienced love versus trauma.

I am learning that God uses every opportunity to grow us spiritually to His character. As we are traveling on our journey, how great is our opportunity to demonstrate God's love and character for our children by how we parent them! Showing them God's heart for them by how we treat them, how we listen to them, and how we protect them. You must block out what you see with your eyes. God always speaks to our potential. It requires patience, long-suffering, and all segments of the Fruit of the Spirit, to look beyond what you see and tap into what's possible and what God sees.

We must follow the pattern of God. God spoke to the Earth without form in Genesis and called those things that are not as though they were. Abraham, known as the father of Faith, also followed the same pattern. Romans 4:17 states, "As it is written: I have made thee a father of many nations, before him whom he believed, even God, who quickeneth the dead, and called those things which be not as though they were." Abraham believed and spoke differently than he saw. Verses 18-19 continue by describing the tenacity of Abraham "who against hope believed in hope, that he might become the father of many nations, according to that which was spoken, So shall thy seed be. And being not weak in faith, he considered not his own body now dead, when he was about a hundred years old, neither yet the deadness of Sarah's womb." Abraham stood on the promises of God and believed differently than what he saw in the natural. According to verses 20-21, "He staggered not at the promise of God through unbelief; but was strong in faith, giving glory to God; And being fully persuaded that, what he had promised he was able also to perform." Abraham was confident that God's promises would come to past. Verses 23-24 states that this was not written for Abraham's sake only "but for us also" through our belief through God's promises and Jesus' deliverance. We have the opportunity to follow the same pattern as Abraham.

We must believe and then speak to activate God's promises. Speaking with purpose is an act of declaring. Declare means "to say something in a solemn and emphatic manner." Declaring God's word aligns our hearts with God's promises and God's will. There is power in speaking God's word. It shows that we are not staggering at the promises of God through unbelief and we are giving glory to God.

The word "decree" is found 55 times in the KJV Bible. Decree, according to the New Oxford American Dictionary, means an official order issued by a legal authority. As Christian believers, we have delegated, legal authority through Jesus Christ. When we decree, we are aligning with truths from the Word of God and from God's heart to be truths in the Earth for our situation.

According to Job 22:28, "Thou shalt also decree a thing and it shall be established unto thee: and the light shall shine upon thy ways."

We have the authority to speak life to our situations; Proverbs 18:21 states, "Death and Life are in the power of the tongue: and they that love it shall eat the fruit thereof." There is a choice. So, let's declare and decree life in our parenting journey. When you speak out loud you also are hearing your voice and we know faith comes by hearing (Hebrews 11:1). Without faith it is impossible to please God. In the model of God in the book of Genesis, God spoke out loud a decree to create, and then He saw what he decreed.

We are made in the image of God and God has given us the authority to declare and decree. Think of "declare and decree" as declaring is saying and decreeing is applying the say to your situation. Below, are some statements I used to declare and decree, in our parenting journey, based on the word of God and our situations.

Declare and Decree:

- We thank you for us winning through Christ who loves us. No weapon formed against us shall prosper as this is our heritage according to Isaiah 54:17.
- My child <name> will have all of their needs met. For according to Philippians 4:19 "But my God shall supply all your need according to his riches in glory by Christ Jesus."
- My child <name> will be like a tree planted by the rivers of water, that bring forth fruit in season, shall not wither, and whatsoever <name> does shall prosper according to Psalm 1:3.

- My child <name> will learn the processes to help <him/her> move from a place of fear to a place of love. For according to II Timothy 1:7, God has not given the spirit of fear but of power, love, and a sound mind.
- My child <name> shall be fruitful in social interactions and environments. We have the resources we need to help strengthen any identified and unidentified needs according to Philippians 4:19.
- <Name> is surrounded by positive influences and friends. For according to Proverbs 27:9, a sweet friendship refreshes the soul.
- <Name> has a complete understanding of <his/her> value and of God. We decree understanding of <his/her> unique beauty and purpose. For according to Jeremiah 29:11, you have plans to prosper our child and not to harm <him/her>. You have plans to give our child a future. According to, Psalm 139:14, our child is fearfully and wonderfully made.
- <Name> has a great purpose as <he/she> was called to God's purpose and grace before the world began according to II Timothy 1:9.
- Lord, help us to speak up and advocate for our child, <name>. Proverbs 31:9 declares "Open thy mouth, judge righteously, and plead the cause of the poor and needy."

When we were going through circumstances, what were we needing in each area? Sometimes we did not know. However, prayer was foundational. Prayer is like a sincere conversation with God. He already knows where you are in your journey. Stormie Omartian summarizes that "when we don't pray, it's like sitting on the side-lines watching our children in a war zone getting shot at from every angle."[29] As a Christian, prayer is a tool of strength and empowerment. We are grabbing hold of the promises of God. We are declaring these promises for our lives and the lives of our children. There are known negative challenges that impact neurodivergent people from anxiety, and suicidal thoughts, to depression. This is the time that we can pray against these challenges and for the proper support for our child. We are in a battle for our child's God-given purpose.

These prayers are written as if parents are praying together for their children. If you are a single parent, these prayers are still powerful for you.

PRAYER FOR PATIENCE

Lord, help us to be patient parents. Give us the understanding to wait and not rush to conclusions. We lay down all of our expectations and come into agreement with Your expectations. Help us to be curious explorers of our child (child's name) and our child's environment. You have and will equip us with all that we need. Thank you for sending your strength. Help us to rest in your truth and not to be anxious. We cast our cares unto you according to I Peter 5:7. Help us not to be discouraged by what we see now but focus on what's possible through this journey. Keep our expectations high for Your promises manifesting in our life. Help us not be quick to anger when behaviors and situations present. We believe You, Lord. We know that the Holy Spirit is working with us and through us on this journey. We will not be weary in well doing. We will see the evidence of the Fruit of the Spirit for our children and family by staying in Your presence. Thank You for Your grace and favor. Amen.

Meditating Bible Verses:

- But if we hope for that we see not, then do we with patience wait for it. — Romans 8:25
- Rejoicing in hope; patient in tribulation; continuing instant in prayer. — Romans 12:12
- Better is the end of a thing than the beginning thereof: and the patient in spirit is better than the proud in spirit. — Ecclesiastes 7:8
- I waited patiently for the Lord; and he inclined unto me, and heard my cry. He brought me up also out of a horrible pit, out of the miry clay, and set my feet upon a rock, and established my goings. And he hath put a new song in my mouth, even praise unto our God: many shall see it, and fear, and shall trust in the Lord. — Psalms 40:1-3

PRAYER FOR WISDOM

Lord, we have tried it our way. Please guide us to the resources that can help us to navigate the next steps. We pray for Your wisdom to be imparted to us as parents. Provide us clarity in the small things. Provide knowledge of how the small things may be impacting our child and the big things. We know You have our best interests at heart and these children were not given to us to fail. Lord, when we feel powerless in this journey and ask "why me?" Help us to declare "why not me?" Help us to embrace the journey. For You are with us. Through You, the impossible is made possible. Amen.

Meditating Bible Verses:

- Great is our Lord, and of great power: His understanding is infinite. — Psalm 147:5
- If any of you lack wisdom, let him ask of God, who giveth to all men liberally, and upbraideth not; and it shall be given him. — James 1:5
- Be careful for nothing; but in every thing by prayer and supplication with thanksgiving let your requests be made known unto God. — Philippians 4:6

PRAYER FOR JOY

Lord, we pray for joy. Help us to find a moment that we can be free. Free to forget our future and to forget our past. A moment to be with You and to just be who You made us to be. Let us rest in Your strength for we know that the joy of our Lord is our strength.

Help us to be present in the now. Help us to experience joy now. Help us to enjoy every moment now with our child(ren) and family. Thank you, God, for freedom. Thank you, God, for peace. Amen.

Meditating Bible Verse:

- He giveth power to the faint, and to them that have no might he increaseth strength. — Isaiah 40:29
- Restore unto me the joy of thy salvation; and uphold me with thy free spirit. — Psalms 51:12
- My soul shall be satisfied as with marrow and fatness; and my mouth shall praise thee with joyful lips. — Psalms 63:5

PRAYER FOR OUR CHILD'S PURPOSE

Lord, we pray for Your purpose to be revealed for us as parents and for our children. When we lack clarity, help us to remember that we are grounded in You. Help us to be stewards of nurturing our children's gifts and strengths, for we know these are part of their purpose. May we be filled with the knowledge of Your will as in Colossians 1:9. Help us to demonstrate that You have a purpose for all types of people even those that are differently wired. Help the works of God to be displayed in us and our children. Help us to be fruitful in every good work according to Colossians 1:10. May You be pleased with our lives and works. Amen.

Meditating Bible Verses:

- Lo, children are an heritage of the Lord: and the fruit of the womb is his reward. — Psalm 127:3
- As arrows are in the hand of a mighty man; so are children of the youth. — Psalm 127:4
- Happy is the man that hath his quiver full of them: they shall not be ashamed, but they shall speak with the enemies in the gate. — Psalm 127:5
- For I know the thoughts that I think toward you, saith the Lord, thoughts of peace, and not of evil, to give you an expected end. —Jeremiah 29:11

PRAYER FOR COMMUNITY

Lord, we pray for us to be connected to the right community. Help us to feel welcome with a sense of belonging— for us and our child.

Although we may feel lonely, help us to focus on the fact that we are not alone. Help us to build a peer community of friends for our children. Give our child friends that are accepting of who <he/she> is. Give our child friends that do not bully or belittle. Friends that have your character of love. Amen.

Meditating Bible Verses:

- A friend loves at all times, and a brother is born for a time of adversity. — Proverbs 17:17
- As iron sharpens iron, so one person sharpens another. — Proverbs 27:17
- Each of you should use whatever gift you have received to serve others, as faithful stewards of God's grace in its various forms. — I Peter 4:10

PRAYER FOR LOVE

Lord, we pray for us to know the fullness of Your love. For we know that perfect love casts away fear. Help us not to be afraid of how we are operating in our life as parents but to rest in your love.

Help our homes to be full of Your love. Help all that enter our homes to feel Your love. Help our children to know that we love them through our actions, our words, and our home environment. Amen.

Meditating Bible Verses:

- Love is patient, love is kind. It does not envy, it does not boast, it is not proud. It does not dishonor others, it is not self-seeking, it is not easily angered, it keeps no record of wrongs. — I Corinthians 13:4-5 (NIV)

- There is no fear in love; but perfect love casteth out fear; because fear hath torment. He that feareth is not made perfect in love. — I John 4:18
- That their hearts might be comforted, being knit together in love, and unto all riches of the full assurance of understanding, to the acknowledgment of the mystery of God, and of the Father, and of Christ —Colossians 2:2

PRAYER FOR PEACE

Lord, we pray for Your peace that surpasses all understanding to rest in our lives. When we feel tossed to and fro, we pray for us to be still and know that you are God. We pray for stillness in our minds and our heart. When we feel incapable, Lord remind us that we are capable. When we feel helpless, Lord remind us that we are help full. When we need a moment, help us realize that we are entitled to it. We will enjoy your creations and marvel at how you take care of the birds and know You will take care of us. This peace, Your peace, will become our foundation for today. Amen.

Meditating Bible Verse:

- And the peace of God, which passeth all understanding, shall keep your hearts and minds through Christ Jesus. — Philippians 4:7
- But seek ye first the kingdom of God, and his righteousness; and all these things shall be added unto you. — Matthew 6:33

- And he answered, Fear not: for they that be with us are more than they that be with them. — II Kings 6:16

ENCOURAGING BIBLE VERSES

- I can do all things through Christ which strengtheneth me. — Philippians 4:13
- But they that wait upon the Lord shall renew their strength; they shall mount up with wings as eagles; they shall run, and not be weary; and they shall walk, and not faint. — Isaiah 40:31
- Train up a child in the way he should go: and when he is old, he will not depart from it. — Proverbs 22:6
- Have not I commanded thee? Be strong and of a good courage; be not afraid, neither be thou dismayed: for the Lord thy God is with thee whithersoever thou goest. — Joshua 1:9
- Finally, brethren, whatsoever things are true, whatsoever things are honest, whatsoever things are just, whatsoever things are pure, whatsoever things are lovely, whatsoever things are of good report; if there be any virtue, and if there be any praise, think on these things. — Philippians 4:8
- For God hath not given us the spirit of fear; but of power, and of love, and of a sound mind. — II Timothy 1:7
- But to do good and to communicate forget not: for with such sacrifices God is well pleased. — Hebrews 13:16
- I will praise thee; for I am fearfully and wonderfully made: marvelous are thy works; and that my soul knoweth right well. — Psalm 139:14

RECOMMENDED BOOKS

Praying Circles Around Your Children by Mark Batterson
The Power of a Praying Parent by Stormie Omartian

GROWTH KEYS: REWIRING YOUR FAITH

1. God is the answer.
2. Have Gratitude.
3. Pray, Decree, and Declare.

Inspiring Quotes

A prayer, it seems to me, implies a promise as well as a request; at the highest level, prayer not only is supplication for strength and guidance, but also becomes an affirmation of life and thus a reverent praise of God. — Walt Disney

Faith isn't the ability to believe long and far into the misty future. It's simply taking God at His Word and taking the next step. — Joni Erickson Tada

Gratitude can transform common days into thanksgivings, turn routine jobs into joy, and change ordinary opportunities into blessings. — William Arthur Ward

Gratitude and attitude are not challenges; they are choices. — Robert Braathe

I don't want my children to be what I want them to be. I want them to become everything God created them to be. — Jon Gordon

Reflecting Questions

- How has your faith been rewired through your journey?
- What additional decrees would you add to your parenting journey?

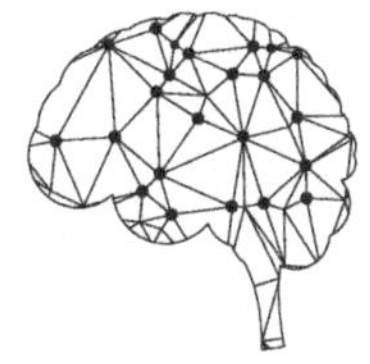

ACKNOWLEDGEMENTS

Writing a book about a personal journey is harder than I thought. Living and parenting a neurodiverse journey is difficult. It requires a village. I want to take a moment to thank some of our key village members. I want to thank every family member, friend, teacher, principal, administrator, bus driver, doctor, therapist, psychologist, and psychiatrist that supported us along the way.

A few of you were a beacon of light when we were at our darkest — thank you. God sent you along at just the right moment. Many of you honored us by asking us if we are ok and offering an ear or advice. Thank you for seeing us through it all.

To all of you reading, thank you. To stay connected or to share how this book may have impacted you, please reach out to nakia@seebeyondconsulting.com or connect to the Facebook community Rewired Parenting.

NOTES

1 Neurodivergent, neurodiversity, and neurotypical: a guide to the terms, https://thebraincharity.org.uk/neurodiversegence-and-neurodiversity-explaining-the-terms/. Accessed 8 July 2022.

2 John N. Costantino et al., Timing of the Diagnosis of Autism in African American Children, Pediatrics (Official Journal of the American Academy of Pediatrics, 2020), https://d2dxtcm9g2oro2.cloudfront.net/wp-content/uploads/2020/10/02133345/diagnosis-disparities-webinar.pdf.

3 John N. Costantino et al., Timing of the Diagnosis of Autism in African American Children, Pediatrics (Official Journal of the American Academy of Pediatrics, September 2020), https://publications.aap.org/pediatrics/article/146/3/e20193629/77116/Timing-of-the-Diagnosis-of-Autism-in-African.

4 Marina Sarris, Are Girls With Autism Hiding in Plain Sight?, Discover Spark (Spark), https://sparkforautism.org/discover_article/are-girls-with-autism-hiding-in-plain-sight/.

5 "Wiring, N. (In electrical engineering)," https://www.collinsdictionary.com/us/dictionary/english/wiring. Accessed 31 December 2021.

6 The Brain from Top to Bottom, https://thebrain.mcgill.ca/flash/d/d_01/d_01_cr/d_01_cr_fon/d_01_cr_fon.html, Accessed 31 December 2021.

7 Dr. Carol S. Dweck, Mindset - Changing the Way You Think to Fulfil your Potential, (Robinson, 2017)

8 Dave Clark, Who Wrote the Software Running in Your Head?, (TimesNews) December 30, 2021, https://www.timesnews.net/opinion/blogs/who-wrote-the-software-running-in-your-head/article_f2b4bc5a-681d-11ec-ae7e-1f2039af4eb4.html. Accessed 31 December 2021.

9 Harsha G, Elon Musk shared an infographic about what every child should learn, (InElectricVehicle) December 28, 2021, https://inelectricvehicle.com/news/elon-musk-shared-an-infographic-about-what-every-child-should-learn/.

10 "Celebrate," https://collinsdictionary.com/us/dictionary/english/celebrate, Accessed 31 December 2021.

11 "Celebrate," https://britannica.com/dictionary/celebrate, Accessed 31 December 2021.

12 "Praise," https://www.merriam-webster.com/dictionary/praise, Accessed 31 December 2021.

13 "Commend," https://www.merriam-webster.com/dictionary/commend, Accessed 31 December 2021.

14 Christine Comaford, Are You Getting Enough Hugs?, (Forbes) August 22, 2022, https://www.forbes.com/sites/christinecomaford/2020/08/22/are-you-getting-enough-hugs/?sh=2b43c6b868da. Accessed 31 December 2021.

15 Mary C. Garvey, But I Am a Child - The Adultification of Black Girls and Implications for Early Childhood, (Institute for Child Success) March 21, 2021, http://www.instituteforchildsuccess.org/but-i-am-a-child-the-adultification-of-black-girls-and-implications-for-ealy-childhood/

16 "Disciplining," https://www.merriam-webster.com/dictionary/disciplining, Accessed 8 July 2022.

17 Ryan Wexelblatt, What Parents Misunderstood About Executive Function, (Additude Inside the ADHD Mind) December 13, 2021,

https://www.additudemag.com/executive-function-adhd-kids-lagging-skills/. Accessed 5 March 2022.

18 Kendra Cherry, How the Visual Cliff Tested Babies' Depth Perception, (verywellmind) November 20, 2020, https://www.verywellmind.com/what-is-a-visual-cliff-2796010/. Access 21 June 2022.

19 James F. Sorce, Robert N. Emde, Jospeh Campos, and Mary D. Klinnert, Maternal emotional signaling: Its effect on the visual cliff behavior of 1-year-olds. Developmental Psychology, 21(1), 195-200

20 "Resilience," https://www.merriam-webster.com/dictionary/resilience, Accessed 26 June 2022.

21 "Grace," https://www.merriam-webster.com/dictionary/grace, Accessed 31 December 2021.

22 "Advocate," https://collinsdictionary.com/us/dictionary/english/advocate, Accessed 17 December 2022.

23 "Advocate," https://www.merriam-webster.com/dictionary/advocate, Accessed 17 July 2022.

24 Anna Brown, "LinkedIn lets users add 'dyslexic thinking' as a skill," (ContentGrip.) April 11, 2022, https://contentgrip.com/linkedin-dyslexic-thinking-skill/. Accessed 9 July 2022.

25 Suzie Glassman, "Why Poor Students Make Great Entrepreneurs," (Entrepreneur's Handbook) October 18, 2020, https://entrepreneurshandbook.co/why-poor-students-make-greate-entrepreneurs-689a2a60c9c3. Accessed 9 July 2022.

26 "Environment," https://www.britannica.com/dictionary/environment, Accessed 2 May 2022

27 Robert Browning, From 'Paracelsus', (Famous Poets and Poems) https://famouspoetsandpoems.com/poets/robert_browning/poems/4925, Accessed 31 December 2021.

28 Julie Kiefer, "We are Different": What Black Communities can teach Doctors and Scientists," https://uofuhealth.utah.edu/newsroom/news/2022/04/autism-black-parents.php, Accessed 26 June 2022.

29 Stormie Omartian, The Power of a Praying Parent, Harvest House Publishers, 1995/2005.